A LIFE
WITHOUT
FEAR

A LIFE WITHOUT FEAR

Laura Martin

RUTLEDGE HILL PRESS

Nashville, Tennessee

The information in this book is given in the hope it will help prevent violent crime against women. However, because each situation is different, there are no guarantees that these tactics will work in all situations. Rutledge Hill Press and Laura C. Martin disclaim any and all liability resulting from the use or attempted use of safety precautions or self-defense strategies discussed in this book.

Published in Nashville, Tennessee, by Rutledge Hill Press, Inc., 513 Third Avenue South, Nashville, Tennessee 37210. Distributed in Canada by H. B. Fenn and Company Ltd., 1090 Lorimar Drive, Mississauga, Ontario.

Typography by D&T/Bailey, Inc., Nashville, Tennessee
Design by Harriette Bateman

Library of Congress Cataloging-in-Publication Data

Martin, Laura, 1952–
    A life without fear / Laura Martin.
        p.   cm.
    Includes bibliographical references and index.
    ISBN 1-55853-197-1
    1. Rape—United States.   2. Rape—United States—Prevention.
I. Title.
HV6561.M37   1992
362.88′3—dc20   92-34239
                                                                              CIP

Printed in the United States of America
1 2 3 4 5 6 7 8 — 97 96 95 94 93 92

How much do you know about rape?

1. How often is a woman raped in America? Once every:
   (a) 2 hours   (b) 56 minutes   (c) 10 minutes   (d) 46 seconds
2. How many women in America have been raped?
   (a) one out of 8   (b) one out of 12   (c) one out of 15   (d) one out of 20
3. How many women knew the men that raped them?
   (a) 10%   (b) 25%   (c) 60%   (d) 80%
4. How many women have been the victim of rape or attempted rape while attending college?
   (a) 5%   (b) 15%   (c) 25%   (d) 50%
5. Sixty-one percent of the women raped in this country were:
   (a) under the age of 17   (b) ages 17-29   (c) ages 30-45   (d) over 45
6. How many rapes were reported to the police?
   (a) 100%   (b) 84%   (c) 50%   (d) 16%
7. What percentage of college women who had been raped expected to be raped again?
   (a) 0%   (b) 12%   (c) 27%   (d) 42%
8. Under what circumstances is it justifiable for a man to force himself sexually on a woman?
   (a) if she's drunk and won't remember anyway
   (b) if she gets him so aroused he can't control himself
   (c) if she goes willingly to his home, promises him sex, and then changes her mind
   (d) all of the above
   (e) none of the above
9. When is it justifiable for a woman to fight back physically?
   (a) never
   (b) if a man stares at her
   (c) if a man makes a suggestive remark
   (d) if a man verbally threatens her
   (e) if a man physically restrains her and she feels that she is in danger.
10. Because women are generally smaller and weaker than men, fighting back physically is not the most practical response.
    True   False
11. What are the best strategies that a woman can use against an attacker?
    (a) pleading, crying, trying to get him to see her as a human
    (b) doing exactly what he says and trying to please him so she will not make him more angry
    (c) fighting back physically and yelling, acting powerful and assertive
    (d) keeping quiet and hoping he will go away
12. Rape is *not* an inevitable part of a woman's life. There are many things that she can do to lessen her chances of being attacked.
    True   False

Answers on next page

To my daughter Cameron
and to the daughters
of mothers everywhere

Special thanks also goes to:
my sister for her courage in facing her tragedy
and sharing her triumph, Jan Ahlund for her
friendship and support throughout the project,
Sally McMillan for her belief in the book
and her untiring persistance in making it work,
Peggy Brown for her knowledge and expertise,
Larry Stone of Rutledge Hill Press
for his clear vision and unfailing support

Additional thanks goes to:
Joey and Sheldon Imperatori—Imperatori Karate
the physical education staff of Westminster Schools
Wendy Palmer Patterson
Dr. Shelley Neiderbach

Answers to questions on previous page:
1. (d) 2. (a) 3. (d) 4. (c) 5. (a) 6. (d) 7. (d) 8. (e) 9. (e)
10. False 11. (c) 12. True

Contents

7

★ Helping As a Community
★ Helping As a State
★ Helping As a Nation

Part Two
Survival Skills

Introduction

April 30, 1992

It's early Thursday morning and I'm sitting sipping coffee, watching the flowers in my garden catch the early sunlight. The children left for school in their usual flurry of happy chaos. The house is quiet, and I wait for that old familiar feeling of contentment to wash over me. But in my heart I know it won't happen today.

I look at my desk, scanning the titles of the books—*Stopping Rape, Talking with Kids about Date Rape, I Never Called It Rape*—and I want to cry. In a fit of anger I have the impulse to fling them out the window and bury myself in the safe cocoon of my garden. I want to write of golden petals and fragrant blossoms. I want to forget about violence and rage and the tragedy of what happens to so many women and girls. But I know I can't. I know too much to turn my back.

I know that 683,000 rapes occurred in the United States last year, nearly two-thirds of them to girls under the age of seventeen. These girls experience the reality of a brutal world before they have a chance to grow up. Having suffered the horrors of a rape, they will endure years of nightmares while they deserve to be enjoying the blissful innocence of childhood.

I look at our daughters and shout, No way! But I know that the possibility exists. It could be a teacher or a coach or someone they meet at school. Or a friend of the family, or an older relative.

I look at senior girls getting ready to go to college and know that, according to statistics, one out of every four will be sexually assaulted or raped during her college years.

I look at my friends and realize that chances are good that at least one of us will be raped sometime during our lives.

So what do we do? Wrap our children in a soft blanket and keep them home? Stay home ourselves hiding behind the shutters? Become so paranoid about our safety that we all fear to face the world?

Imagining a life without fear is a truly different idea for most women, an idea we consider with awe and wonder. Is it possible?

It is not necessary for us to become prisoners of our fear, for there are things that we can do. A vast number of rapes are preventable. Education is the key. We need to learn why rapes occur, why certain women are chosen as victims, and what we can do to prevent becoming victims. We must learn to believe in ourselves and in our right to the safety and privacy of our bodies. There will never be enough law enforcement officers, campus patrols, or burglar alarms to keep us safe. For women to experience a life without fear will require nothing short of radical changes in society.

To help stop the epidemic of rape in America, women must work together; and we need help. We need politicians. We need business and religious leaders. We need educators. We need journalists. We need the collective energy and creativity of everyone we can reach. The problem is evident, and the solution is becoming more and more clear.

Girls and women must learn to take control of their own lives, to speak assertively about their basic rights, and, if necessary, to fight for these rights. We must change the ways we think, for taking control is alien to the way many of us were raised or are now raising our daughters.

We must change the expectations and exploitations of sex in our culture. Men and boys must know *and understand* that rape is not justifiable under any circumstances. To force a woman to have sex without her consent, no matter where she is, what she is wearing, or how much she has been drinking, is a crime against humanity and against the laws of our nation.

Significant changes will take place only when men and women together learn to communicate more clearly, to understand each other more fully, and to develop relationships based on trust, respect, and love.

A LIFE
WITHOUT
FEAR

Part One

What You Need to Know About Rape— Whether You Want To or Not

None of us really wants to learn about rape. It is a subject about which we would just as soon know nothing, but we have no choice. The epidemic of rape has touched us all. It has filled us with fear—rightly so—for a woman is not safe in the society in which we live.

To understand what we can do about rape, we first need to understand what rape is, what causes men to rape women, and exactly how prevalent the problem is.

We need to know why it is difficult for women to defend themselves and how our culture and upbringing have contributed to this difficulty. It is important for us to know exactly what date rape and acquaintance rape are and how to deal with someone who has been raped.

Most tragically of all, we need to face the reality that thousands of children under the age of eleven are raped every year. As loving, caring individuals, it is our responsibility first to educate ourselves and then to commit ourselves to helping stop the epidemic of rape.

1

A Life with Fear

The phone rang on Valentine's Day 1984. When I answered, I hardly recognized my mother's voice.

"Something terrible has happened," she told me, her voice quivering. "Your sister has been raped."

My sister? No. I simply could not believe it. But my mother's wrenching sobs and my sister's haunted eyes told me this was no story, no mistake, but a tragedy.

Bit by bit the story came out. My sister was a teacher for the city school system. When she arrived early that morning at her inner-city school, a man wearing a ski mask grabbed her arm, put a gun to her head, and demanded that she get back in her car and drive to a nearby abandoned house. There he raped her and disappeared.

Fear, disbelief, and shock settled upon us, and then finally outrage and anger. How dare someone violate my sister like that! How dare someone strip her of her privacy, hurt her physically, and leave her to carry on her life as if nothing had happened!

The Statistics Are Frightening

Unfortunately, today those emotions are felt by an astounding number of families throughout the United States. In 1992 the National Victim Center and the Crime Victims Research and Treatment Center conducted a study on rape in America. Their findings were grim—and startling because these new figures on rape were dramatically higher than those previously reported by the Department of Justice and FBI. According to this new study, one out of every eight women in this country has been raped. This is a rate of 683,000 rapes every year. In less time than it took you to read the first page of this book, somewhere in America a woman was raped. Every 46 seconds—night and day, in every kind of community imaginable—a woman is raped. This is no longer a crime of the inner city, no longer a crime that only happens to "someone else." Rape is a crime that happens with such alarming frequency and terrifying regularity that it touches all of our lives.

Rape can happen to any of us. For girls going off to college, the statistics are particularly grim. Imagine four girls getting together before they leave for college. They may sit at lunch, talking about how excited they are about going away for the first time, and about how their lives are really just beginning. According to statistics, one of the four will be the victim of rape or attempted rape during her college career, probably during her freshman year. Her life will most likely be changed forever. Rape is not something that can easily be forgotten.

Rape knows no age limit. Thousands of little girls who do not even know what sex is are raped. A full 29 percent of all rape victims are under the age of eleven. Thirty-two percent of all rape victims are between the ages of eleven and seventeen.

The offender could be a stepfather, an older brother, or a father; it could be a teacher or a coach. He is almost always someone older, someone that these little girls trust. And after they are raped, chances are, they will be raped over and over again. Most incidences of incest rape occur over long periods of time, sometimes months, sometimes even years.

We prefer to think of rape as an act committed by a crazy stranger in a dark alley in a city far from where we live. That just isn't true. Eight out of ten girls and women knew the men that raped them. Sometimes it is men whom we go to school with. Sometimes it is someone known only casually.

One friend of mine—recently divorced—decided she really

needed to get out more. She went to a dance club with some friends and met a man that she knew casually at her work. They left the club and went for a drink, and then he took her home. She asked him in, and he came willingly. As soon as the door was closed, he started fondling her and then threatened to hit her as she tried to stop him. Scared to death, she quit struggling and made no noise as he raped her. She did not report it to the police, tried to avoid the man at work, and for months didn't tell anyone. She felt that it was somehow her fault because she had invited him to her home.

My friend's reaction is typical. Fully 84 percent of rape victims do not report the crime to police. Sixty-nine percent fear being blamed by others for somehow causing the rape.

According to the legal definition, rape is vaginal, oral, or anal penetration without the consent or through the use of force or threat of force.

Though boys and men can be rape victims, the vast majority of victims are women. Rape has become a crime against women of almost epidemic proportions, but it must be addressed by men and women and stopped, for it strikes at the very roots of our culture.

Myths About Rape

What allows this epidemic to continue? Part of the answer lies in the miscommunication that exists about rape. In spite of its widespread occurrence, many people—men and women—do not understand exactly what rape is and why it occurs.

Many men who meet the legal definition of a rapist insist they have raped no one. The underlying attitude among many men and women is that if certain situations exist, forced intercourse is justifiable.

Anna was a freshman at a small university in the Midwest. She had dieted all summer getting ready for college, and for the first time in her life, she had a figure to be proud of. She and a friend decided to go to a party for the football players, and Anna put on a tight tank top and a miniskirt. She felt a little self-conscious, but she received so much attention from boys that she soon got used to it. One of the football players asked her to go for a walk and, flushed with excitement, Anna readily agreed. They were in a secluded part of the campus when he told her to lie down. When she refused, he threw her to the ground, telling her that she'd been "asking for it" all night. Otherwise, why would she dress like that?

When she accused him of rape, he just laughed and told her that everyone knew that she had dressed like a hooker for the party. She got what she asked for.

It is a common fallacy that if a woman dresses suggestively or goes to an isolated spot with a man, she is really asking for sex.

Another common misconception about sex and rape is that many men and boys believe that "when she says no, she really means yes." Unfortunately, this myth is perpetuated by girls and women who do not always clearly communicate their feelings about having sex. If a woman plays coy or is too embarrassed or shy to speak her mind, she reinforces this myth and brings danger to us all.

Still another falsehood about rape is that if a victim is not beaten up, cut, or bruised, or shows no other signs of a struggle, she must not have been raped. Some of the saddest stories come from girls who seek help after a rape only to be turned away by authorities or family members who callously tell them they didn't look like they'd been raped.

Boys and men often believe that raping a woman is justifiable if she sexually teases and arouses them. A man might even tell her that he has "blue balls," a myth that if a man is sexually aroused and does not have intercourse, his testicles will turn blue. Many men believe that if they are aroused, they cannot control themselves, therefore making forced sexual intercourse justifiable.

Why Is Rape So Prevalent?

What fosters these attitudes? What makes men think they are not responsible for their actions if they are sexually aroused? What makes women accept the idea that if they agree to go to an isolated spot with a guy, they deserve to be raped? How did communication between men and women get so confused that a man would think a woman really wanted sex even though she was shouting "No!"

Many of the answers lie in how our society views rape and sex. Rape is a familiar term these days, the object of many jokes and the topic of many songs, a common theme in the daytime soap operas watched by millions of Americans every day.

The frequency of sexual assault is a result, in part, of a barrage of violence from television, movies, and even the daily news. With rape such a common topic, we are becoming desensitized to the horrors of this criminal act.

Much of the music popular with young people refers casually to rape and violence as everyday occurrences. Kids are surrounded by soft-core pornography. They see it on television; they see it in advertising; they see it at the movies. In Hollywood sex is often accompanied by violence, and in a kid's eyes, the two may soon become inseparable. If boys learn about the facts of life by watching actors and actresses, they are going to come away with skewed ideas of a healthy relationship.

Adults, also, are greatly influenced by the shower of sexual themes that come to us through television and film. Rarely do we see strong, independent women who develop loving, healthy relationships with men. Too often the heroine is either sweet, submissive, and lost without a man, or so hard and bitchy she is impossible for anyone to love. Movies like *Gone With the Wind* show the heroine essentially raped and then display her as being madly in love with her attacker the next morning. This sends confusing messages to men and women of all ages.

The freedom and choices at our colleges and universities are sometimes overwhelming today. Many college dormitories are completely coed now, the men and women sometimes only separated by rooms. Many fraternities and sororities no longer have house mothers, and the result is a tremendous increase of opportunities for young men and women to be together in isolated situations. The epidemic of rape on our college campuses indicates that this situation needs to be examined closely.

Perhaps one of the most important factors that leads to rape and sexual violence is the way we teach our children to view men and women and sexual relationships in our society. Boys are taught to be strong and aggressive; girls are taught to be sweet and submissive; and both are taught that fulfilling these roles will bring them happiness.

At the brink of maturity many boys are taught that sex is a commodity—the more they get, the more macho they will be. The very language many males use to describe sex indicates how widespread this is: "Did you get some?" "Did you score?" "Look at that piece of ass!" Sex as a commodity leads to the attitude that if a couple is out on a date and the man pays for the food and entertainment, he deserves to be paid back with sexual favors. Therefore he may choose his date because of the sex he may get from her, not because of the kind of person she is.

His interest is in sexual gratification, not in the person. With this dehumanizing, any means of getting sex seems justified to some of these individuals—even rape. And this brings fear to our hearts.

The Fear Touches Us All

Fear among women in this country is rampant. We are scared—with good reason—for we are not safe. Even if we have never experienced sexual assault, the fear of such has touched us and influenced the way we lead our lives. We are often tense and nervous when we are on the street; we may choose to stay at home rather than get out at night because we are afraid; we may even routinely check under the bed or in the closet simply because our lives have been invaded by fear. We fear for ourselves, for our sisters, and for our daughters. This fear paralyzes us, keeping us from growing into the women we are capable of becoming.

IN A NUTSHELL

1. The following are statistics about rape in America:
   - Every 46 seconds a woman is raped in America.
   - One in eight women has been raped.
   - 29 percent of all rape victims are younger than eleven years old.
   - 32 percent of all rape victims are between the ages of eleven and seventeen.
   - Eight out of ten women know their attacker.
   - There are a total of 683,000 rapes in America every year.
   - 84 percent of rape victims do not report the crime to the police.
2. Myths and untruths about rape persist, including:
   - If a woman dresses suggestively, she must be asking for sex.
   - If a woman agrees to go to an isolated spot with a man, she deserves to be raped.
   - It is not really rape if the woman is not a virgin or if she is not cut, bruised, or beaten up.
   - If a man pays for everything, a woman owes him sex.
   - If a woman teases a man and gets him aroused, he is not responsible for his actions because he cannot control himself.

2

Rapists and Rape Victims

Janice was so tired she didn't think she could carry the tray back to the kitchen. It was the end of the longest day of her life. Slowly she straightened, putting her hand on the small of her back.

"You'll get used to it." Martha's gravelly voice was kind.

Janice turned to the older girl beside her. "I don't know if I can take it. I've never been so tired in my life." It was her first day at the little downtown café. She had been there since noon, waiting tables, clearing away dishes, running back and forth between the dining room and the kitchen. She knew she had to be able to take it. She and her best friend had just moved to the city and had rented a small apartment.

As she was finally getting her coat to go home, she stopped to say goodnight to Martha. She could be pretty, Janice thought, if she didn't look so discouraged all the time.

Martha sighed and put out her cigarette. "Well, we made it through another day, thank the Lord." She shuffled to her feet. "Come on, let's walk out together. You know this city's full of monsters."

Janice looked uneasy, and her heart did a little leap within her.

"Have you ever had trouble?" she asked, her voice squeaking a little.

Martha's eyes clouded over, and her shoulders slumped forward. "Yeah, I've been raped twice, damn them."

Janice was shocked. "Twice! My God, Martha, what happened?"

She looked away again. "Not much. Last time some guy grabbed me on the street and told me not to scream or he would hurt me. Nothing you can do about it. I guess it's just a part of living in the city."

Janice still couldn't believe it. All of a sudden the city did not seem so magical after all. "Well, come on, at least we can walk out together."

From the shadows the man had been watching the two waitresses for about an hour. He knew that the café would be closing soon and that the women would be coming out into the street. He was nervous, and his hands twitched as he held the dark ski mask.

As the two women emerged from the door, he slunk across the street and disappeared into the shadows. For two blocks he followed them, keeping far enough behind that they never suspected that he was there. When they came to the first major intersection, they stood chatting for a moment, obviously deciding to go in different directions.

The man looked from one to the other and knew he would have to choose which one to continue to follow. There was really no decision. The pretty one was tired but alert and looked fairly fit. The other one looked as if she was resigned to whatever fate would bring her. Her shoulders were slumped, she shuffled, and the man knew she would not put up a fight.

As Martha turned down Oak Street, the man in the shadows was right behind her.

It was not just a twist of fate that caused the would-be rapist to follow Martha and not Janice. Even though Janice was much prettier, she was not the kind of woman he was looking for. Martha acted like a victim even before she became one. Her entire body language shouted, Well, there's nothing I can do about it, an attitude easily communicated to her attacker.

Is Rape an Inevitable Part of Life?

Women are crying for answers to basic questions. Is rape an inevitable part of being a woman? Is sexual assault a natural part of the male demeanor? Are all women victims? Are all men rapists? Are there things that we can do to prevent a rape from happening?

There are, sadly, more questions than answers. Rape has received tremendous news coverage and has been the subject for numerous national studies and reports. Statistics about rape abound. We know how many women are raped, how often rape occurs, and how old the victims are. What we don't know is *why* so many women are raped. All we can do is speculate and then wonder further why more is not done to prevent these crimes against women.

Some questions are easier to answer than others. First, not all men are rapists, and not all women are victims. There is nothing within the general biological or psychological makeup of men that causes them to be rapists. Likewise, there is nothing inherent within women that predetermines that they will be victims.

To understand why so many women are victims of rape or attempted rape, it is important for us to understand what causes a man to rape, and what can influence the possibility of a rape occurring.

To the rapist, a sexual assault is a matter of power, not sex. It is the desire to control and dominate another human being that compels these men to rape women.

Control is a crucial point of the attack. In the rapist's mind, it is the most important element. A rapist's desire is not for a romantic interlude, but for a situation where he has total control and his power is complete. The rapist relies heavily on the naturally submissive nature of many women that makes them easy to control. The sexual act becomes a weapon of degradation and a means to dominate a woman.

In a date or acquaintance rape situation, the reasons change only slightly. The man may have a greater interest in sex, but certainly not in his partner. A college-age man may be mostly interested in discovering the power he feels when he intimidates a woman by forcing himself on her.

If this is true (and experts from all fields from law enforcement to victim counseling agree that it is), then what a woman *looks* like has little to do with her chances of becoming a victim. If sexual desire drove men to rape, it would be reasonable to assume that the very young and the very old would be safe from the threat of attack.

We know that this is not so. Women and girls of all ages—of all walks of life and of every physical description—have been the victims of rape.

To the rapist, a sexual assault is a matter of power, not sex.

There is nothing remotely flattering about being raped. Women who think that they are so beautiful or so sexy that men cannot control themselves around them must face reality. To a rapist, it doesn't matter what a woman looks like; it only matters that he can control his victim. There is nothing pretty about rape. It is horribly degrading; it is terrifying; and it is painful.

Characteristics of a Rapist

Rapists do not look different from the rest of the male population. Rapists have been tall or short, thin or fat, good looking or not, dark haired or light, or bald. There are no physical characteristics that identify a man as a rapist.

There are many different reasons why some men rape. Many rapists were physically or sexually abused as children or come from broken homes where the mother was abused. Often these men view rape as a way to gain power and control in their lives.

Some rapists may gain control by verbally intimidating the victim, by telling her what to say and how to say it. The amount of physical control a rapist uses may vary from simply holding her down with the weight of his body to sadistic mutilation or even murder.

Joan was getting into her car in a downtown area when she was approached by a man on the street who asked her for money. When she refused him, he put a gun to her head, pushed her into the car, and drove to an isolated spot outside the city. When he finally stopped the car, he demanded that she strip and spent the next several hours making her act out his perverse sexual fantasies. Every time she hesitated, he shot at her feet. Terrified, Joan did as she was told until he finally tired of the game. He beat her up, brutally raped her, and left her in the trunk of her own car.

Neither sexual release nor the idea of sexual pleasure compels these men to rape. They feel a need to dominate, humiliate, and control a victim.

Opportunity and Attitude

A rapist needs two things to carry out an attack: opportunity and a victim. He must find or create an opportunity to commit the attack. He can't very well grab you in the middle of a crowded restaurant, during class, or in the midst of a business meeting, throw you on the floor, and rape you. He's got to get you to a place where there will be no interference or interruptions for at least a short period of time. He has to create that opportunity. He will do this either by attacking women when they are alone in a secluded spot or by taking his victim to such an area. Many things create or destroy an opportunity for an attacker.

Sometimes women are forced to go to an isolated spot at gunpoint or under the threat of other violence to themselves or to someone they love. At other times women will go to a secluded place willingly, particularly if it is a dating situation and they have no reason to be suspicious.

The second thing that a rapist needs is a victim, but not just any victim. A rapist looks for a certain kind of woman. Since his compulsion is for power, he is looking for someone who is easily intimidated, who will cower and grovel under his control. He is looking for someone who has an attitude of weakness and submission and who looks whipped even before he gets to her.

To find a good victim, the rapist will often test out several women, asking for directions, money, or the time of day. The attacker may base his next actions on the kind of response he gets. If the woman is clearly polite to the point of being submissive and nervous to the point of terror, he may take her responses as an indication that she would make an easy victim.

Because we know what a rapist needs, we also know what it takes to avoid rape. Rape is not just a matter of chance. Rape is a preventable crime. We must avoid situations that are likely to give a rapist an opportunity to commit the crime, and we must project an attitude that clearly says "I am not a victim!"

Characteristics of a Victim

In most cases of rape, the attacker is anxious to bully someone into submission, and the more afraid and terrified the victim acts, the more powerful he feels. A woman trained by her culture and encouraged by tradition to be quiet and deferential makes the perfect victim for a sexual assault.

> A rapist will not choose a victim who looks like she will make things difficult for him.

Women are often marked as "easy" victims (easy for the attacker, that is). In the rapist's mind, he will be a figure of power and control. He expects his victim to recognize this power and succumb to it by pleading, begging, and crying for mercy. This, of course, will make him feel even more powerful.

The rapist will usually choose his victim carefully and will select someone who he believes will fill the role of his imagination. A rapist will not choose a victim who looks as though she will make things difficult for him.

Each of us possesses characteristics that could mark us as "easy" victims. While it is impossible to say, "If you do this, you will be raped," it *is* possible to say "If you portray certain characteristics, *you greatly increase your chances of being sexually assaulted.*"

Most studies about rape have shown that while all types of women have been raped, women who are at a greater risk of being sexually assaulted tend to be:

- submissive
- unsure of themselves
- passive
- anxious to please
- easily intimidated
- convinced they could not fight back

Are *You* an Easy Victim?

How you respond to other people and to stressful situations has a great deal to do with your chances of being the victim of sexual assault.

Test yourself by answering the following questions. You might be surprised at some of your answers.

- Do you try to be nice and polite to everyone you meet—stranger or friend—whatever the circumstances?
- Do you sacrifice your wants and needs to keep peace in the family or among friends?
- Do you think it would be impossible for you to scream or make a scene if you needed help?
- Is it so important that you fit in with a group of friends that you sometimes make unwise decisions?
- Are you totally dependent on a man for financial support, for security, or for happiness?
- Do you feel selfish if you take time for yourself?
- When you get scared or nervous, do you "freeze" and do nothing?
- When you walk in public do you appear shy and timid?

If you answered "yes" to most of these questions, you might ask, "But aren't these good characteristics? Isn't that what we're supposed to do? I like to be nice to people! I work hard at keeping peace in the family!"

We have been taught from an early age that it is a woman's responsibility to work on relationships and keep things peaceful and happy at home. But it is these same characteristics that sometimes lead to trouble in the outside world.

If most of your answers were "yes," you might take a good, long look at how you think and what you believe. These may indicate that you lack the self-confidence or self-esteem to fend for yourself and keep yourself safe. *You may show characteristics of an easy victim.*

If you act like a victim, chances are good that you will become a victim.

How Did We Become Such Easy Victims?

Women today grow up believing that somewhere "out there" is a prince charming who will rush into our lives, sweep us off our feet, and make us live happily ever after. If we are only *good* enough, we can catch him. So we spend our lives trying to be good.

Mothers and daughters, culture and tradition have created generations of women who have been encouraged to be sweet and unselfish and to hide their true strength, wisdom, and courage so they might be more pleasing to men.

Unfortunately, this idea is still being perpetuated. Former President Richard Nixon, referring to political wives in the 1992 presidential race, said, "If the wife comes through as being too strong and too intelligent, it makes the husband look like a wimp."

As long as we perpetuate this myth about innocent, helpless women, we will be at risk for our physical and psychological health and safety. It is essential that the "damsel in distress" not wait for her knight in shining armor to come to her rescue, but to learn to wield the sword herself.

Not long ago I gave a series of self-defense workshops to a

group of girls at an exclusive private high school. Most of the girls put forth effort and were obviously enjoying the experience. However, one girl in particular stayed in the back of the class, looking bored and seeming more interested in the chip in her nail polish than in perfecting an elbow strike against a soft target.

Finally my curiosity got the best of me. I approached her and asked if she felt that she could use this basic self-defense move if necessary.

She shrugged. "I don't know, but it doesn't really matter."

I looked puzzled. "Well, what would you use instead?"

She shrugged again. "I won't ever need any of this stuff. I'll always be with my boyfriend or my daddy, and they'll take care of me."

It's so easy to bury our heads and pretend that someone—some fairy godfather—will always be there for us. *But unless we live a life of seclusion, always protected from the basic realities of the world, we must be responsible for our own well being.*

Women's inability to stand up for ourselves—physically, emotionally, or verbally—is in part the reason for such widespread rape. We too often are victims because we don't know how to be assertive and outspoken. We don't know how to fight for our safety and the integrity of our bodies.

Adding to Our Vulnerability

Considering the fact that women are generally smaller and weaker than men and that most of us were raised to be obliging, soft-spoken, and gentle, it is no surprise that so many women are sexually victimized.

But other factors also influence our vulnerability. What makes it worse?

- alcohol and drugs
- trying to fit into a new social situation
- feeling depressed
- a feeling of helplessness

Alcohol and drugs tend to dull the senses, making it difficult to communicate, to sense danger, or to use and coordinate our muscles, all of which are undesirable factors in a stressful or potentially dangerous situation.

According to the *Ms.* magazine survey on date rape, "about 75 percent of the men and at least 55 percent of the women involved in acquaintance rapes had been drinking or taking drugs just before the attack."

Alcohol and drugs slow your reaction time. When intoxicated or stoned, it is harder for you to realize that you are in danger or that the danger is escalating.

Young women on their own for the first time are also a large "at risk" group. At college, or while living away from home for the first time, these women are anxious to test their new independence and to fit into adult situations. These women want desperately to appear worldly and sophisticated and will make tragic judgmental errors concerning drugs, alcohol, and choice of dates.

Trying hard to fit in makes them particularly vulnerable to the people they see as successful. A figure of power, whether he is president of the fraternity, on the football team, or a successful member of the corporation, can easily exert power and pressure on a woman new to the situation.

Even the time of day may influence your ability to project the right attitude. My sister who was raped definitely is not a morning person. Before ten o'clock in the morning, she is not very alert. She was raped early in the morning, when her senses were still groggy from sleep and she was least able to defend herself.

Women are most at risk when they are at an emotional low point and their self-confidence is sagging. These low points may occur after breaking up with a boyfriend or husband, losing a job, or being away from home for the first time. *When you are feeling the lowest is when you need to be most alert to danger.*

When you are depressed, it is easy to slip into a victim mentality where you think that life is dumping on you and nothing that you do matters much anyway.

Perhaps the most tragic cases of rape come from battered

women. These women are usually attacked in their homes by husbands or boyfriends. Because there is often nowhere to run and no place that they feel completely safe, these women often are enveloped by feelings of helplessness.

Studies have shown that laboratory animals that have no effect on their environment eventually give up—they simply quit responding. Humans will do the same thing. Women in abusive relationships often believe they are powerless to change their situation. They are frozen by fear and truly believe there is no way out.

To a lesser degree, all women are frozen by fear. Because we have been taught that we are incapable of taking care of our-selves, we have believed it. We have accepted fear as part of our daily lives.

> **When you are feeling the lowest is when you need to be most alert to danger.**

Rape has been called a man's problem, and many men will say, "We'll take care of it." I disagree. If we wait for men to take care of the problem of rape, we are still depending on them to protect us. Rape is a problem for *all* of us—all genders, all races, all ages. Together we must address it and make whatever changes necessary to stop it. Thoreau said that for every thousand hacking at the leaves of evil, only one is striking at the root. We must all work together to sever the root of this problem.

There are a lot of effective quick fixes such as better lighting, greater numbers of law enforcement officials, and stricter punishment for offenders; but the root of the problem is in how men and women treat each other and the cultural expectations and exploitations of sex. The answer to this problem—like so many problems—lies in love and respect for one another.

IN A NUTSHELL

1. Rape is a matter of power, not sex.
2. Therefore women and girls of all ages, of all walks of life, of all physical descriptions are vulnerable to sexual assault.

3. Two main factors influence the possibility of attack: opportunity and the attitude of the intended victim.
4. Therefore by avoiding situations that would lead to opportunities for a rapist and by changing our attitudes, we can help prevent ourselves from being raped.
5. Outside factors that influence the possibility of our becoming sexual assault victims include alcohol and drugs, trying to fit into a new social situation, feeling depressed, and a general feeling of helplessness.

Using the Exercises in This Book

It is easy to read a book and understand what has been written, but to be able to *use* the information that you have read is something altogether different. Imagine that you have read a book on learning to play tennis. You understand how to grip the racket, how to take a back swing and a follow-through, and how to serve and volley.

Even though you may understand all of this intellectually, if you never pick up a tennis racket, the information is of limited use.

The same is true of keeping yourself safe. You may read about how to vent your anger, how to speak assertively, how to increase your muscle strength or execute an eye strike, but if you never practice these things, your ability to use them when you need them will be severely limited.

The exercises are designed to involve you in preparing for your own safety. They are crucial to your ability to live your life as fully and safely as possible. They are not designed to give you a thinner figure, to help you project a more lovely image, or to be fun. These exercises are designed to save your life. Do them.

Exercise 1

1. List five reasons why you would like to be alive ten years from now.
2. List ten personal qualities that you consider most desirable. Star the ones that you are strongest in. Underline the ones

you would like to work on.

3. List five goals you would like to achieve during the next five years.

4. If you only had a month to live, how would you spend your time? Write it down.

5. Make up a personal mission statement. Include what kind of person you would like to be, your ambitions and goals, and your values and principles.

Exercise 2

Self-esteem is a critical element in successful self-defense. If you are going to do everything possible to save your life and the integrity of your body, then you need to know that *you are precious. You are worth fighting for.*

This reasoning does not come automatically to many of us. Luck and circumstances may have created negative feelings about ourselves that have caused us to lose sight of how important and wonderful we really are.

By saying these statements of affirmation with conviction, we will begin to believe in them, and then in ourselves. Practice saying them in the mirror every day. Add to or substitute statements that are more applicable for you.

1. I love myself just like I am.

2. I am a good person, and I don't have to change to please anyone else.

3. I am a strong, capable, assertive woman.

Exercise 3

Every night before you go to bed, write down on a piece of paper:

I forgive myself for _____ .

Exercise 4

Imagine that you are going to spend the day with your best friend. She has been feeling low lately, and you want to really boost her spirits and help her regain her confidence. Think of all the funny, wonderful, kind things you will say to her and the sweet, nurturing things you will do for her. Now surprise yourself by treating yourself like your best friend. Take a whole day for yourself.

3

Stumbling Blocks to Safety

Frances smiled to herself in the mirror. She had been at college for only two days, and already she had a date! She hardly knew the boy, but that was okay with her. He was a member of one of the best fraternities on campus, and she knew she would have a good time at the party.

Frances was ready and waiting at seven o'clock when William called her dorm room. She hurried down the stairs, a little nervous and greatly excited.

The evening started well. William was attentive, almost overwhelmingly so. As soon as they got to the party, he started pouring drinks, teasing her about being a freshman and new on campus. As she looked around her, Frances was startled to see that she was the only freshman present. She was pleased, but it made her a bit nervous, too. She wished there was someone she knew. She was not used to drinking and was already beginning to feel dizzy, but she wanted desperately to appear like this was just another party—something that she had done often.

Toward midnight the party seemed to be thinning out. William took her arm and suggested that they go upstairs. Just for a few minutes, he told her. "I've had to share you all evening, and I thought it would be nice to have a little time for just us."

Frances was drunk by this time, and all she really wanted to do was go back to the dorm and go to sleep. But through the haze of her mind, she was vaguely flattered that William wanted to get to know her better, so she struggled to her feet and let him lead her upstairs.

When they reached the back bedroom, Frances stopped in the doorway. No one else was in the room, and the only place to sit seemed to be the bed. An alarm went off in the back of her head. She turned to William. "I think I'd better go home," she said, her voice thick and her words slurred.

William pretended not to hear and tightened his grip on her hand. Pushing her into the room, he shut the door behind them. Immediately he started to kiss and fondle her.

Frances tried to pull away, but it was as if her arms were made of lead. She seemed to have no strength. Roughly, William pushed her onto the bed and started pulling down her pants. Frances started crying, telling him no over and over again, but William acted obsessed.

Frances could not believe what was happening to her. Was this what was supposed to happen at fraternity parties? Frances heard people in the next room, but she was hesitant to call out for help. If she screamed now and embarrassed William, she would never be invited to another party—maybe never have another date. So, sobbing uncontrollably, Frances submitted to the rape.

When he was finally through, William pushed himself off her and put his clothes back on. Neither of them said a word as he took her back to her dorm. As Frances fell out of his car, still crying, William waved goodbye. "See you on Monday!" he said and drove off as if nothing out of the ordinary had happened.

Frances's attitude represents one of the major stumbling blocks to staying safe.

Common Stumbling Blocks

Asked to defend themselves, women offer an astounding array of excuses why they cannot do so. They range anywhere from "I'm too uncoordinated" to "I'd never be able to scream" to "I couldn't fight or run, I usually wear tight skirts and high heels."

For just a moment, think about being attacked. Close your eyes and imagine that you are with a man at a party and he has told you he wants to make love with you. He has grabbed your arm and is pushing you out the door toward your car. You have only met this man, and you are terrified that he will rape you. You know there are people in the next room. Could you scream for help and fight to keep from being raped? If you feel that you could not, why not? Do you not want to cause a scene? Are you afraid he will become more violent if you start to struggle? Do you think that he is so much stronger that fighting back would do no good?

The answers to these questions may show you some important things about yourself. They will be the beginning of your personal list of stumbling blocks to safety.

By understanding your own personal nemeses—the things that you feel would keep you from being able to defend yourself—you will begin to overcome these stumbling blocks. Realizing that you can defend yourself is the first step to attaining a life without fear.

Although women have many hidden talents and are capable of tremendous intellectual and physical feats, we are quick to point out the things that we cannot do rather than brag about the ones we can do. Rather than risk failure, we're quick to make up some kind of excuse for why we can't do something.

Whenever I teach a self-defense class, I am amazed at the number of women who spend more time and energy trying to tell me why self-defense won't work than they do learning the basics of staying safe.

If I say, "Don't read a book while you're waiting for the bus," someone will invariably say, "Well, what if I have an exam the next day?"

If I say, "One of your best self-defense weapons is to scratch the attacker across the face," someone will say, "What if I just cut my fingernails?"

If I say, "Run to lights and people," someone will say, "What if I don't see any lights and people?"

There simply are not enough rules to cover every contingency. No responses are guaranteed to work in every situation because every situation is different.

When defending ourselves, it is crucial that we keep the big picture in mind. Emphasize what you *can* do rather than what you can't do. Work on what will work and forget about what won't work.

If you think you can, or you think you can't, you're right.

Stumbling Block 1: Nothing I do makes much of a difference.

Boyce Appel, a psychologist in Atlanta, Georgia, runs a class for corporate executives called Positive Power and Influence. Based on his experiences over many years of counseling and training, he says that *people who do not believe they can make a difference rarely do.*

You can make a difference in every situation you are involved in. In defending yourself, the only way you cannot make a difference is by thinking you can't.

It is essential to remember that you are never defenseless—in any situation—and the attacker is never invulnerable.

If you are a victim, you will always have weapons at your disposal. You have your hands and arms, your feet and legs; you have your body, your voice, and your head. Even if you are bound and gagged, you still have the most important weapon of all, your brain. There is no time when you cannot make a difference, unless you give up.

In his class, Boyce Appel teaches his students to feel more powerful by helping them realize their power potential and their ability to exert influence. Everyone can influence people. It is a skill that lies within us all. To do this most effectively, we need to practice.

Practice using your influence in a safe environment and in a positive way. Choose one person whom you would like to influence. It could be a secretary where you work or maybe a girl who lives down the hall in the dorm. You can make a difference in her life; start paying attention to her. Speak to her when you see her. Compliment her when she looks nice. Ask her about her family. If she looks down, ask her if she's OK. The amount of influence you will have on this person is in direct relation to the amount of *you* you invest in her. If you only speak to her superficially, you will have superficial influence and will not make much of a difference in her life.

If you can truly learn to listen to her, to get involved in her successes and her failures, you will begin to make a difference to her.

There are many different ways for you to influence people. Some of us are logically oriented and want to deal with people and problems analytically (such as, "I know you've been having trouble in math lately, why don't we set up a study schedule so you can work on it from six till eight every morning").

Others are more "feeling" oriented and will go straight to the emotional aspects of a situation ("I know you've been having trouble in math. I'm so sorry. It's tough for me too, but you know, who needs math anyway?")

Some of us are naturally aggressive and will come on fairly strong ("Get off your butt and start studying"). Others are more laid back and quiet and have a more gentle approach ("Maybe if you have a little extra time you could peek at your math book this afternoon").

To influence people and make a difference most effectively, we must learn a variety of approaches, whether we use these to make new friends or to save our lives in a dangerous situation. If we only rely on the approach that feels most comfortable to us, we will run into situations where that approach will not work well. Enlarge your repertoire. Try different approaches.

It is true that in a self-defense situation, you will not have the luxury of knowing exactly which approach will be most effective against an attacker. But if you have made a practice of influencing people—of making a difference in their lives—then you will be skilled at reading people and knowing which approaches work best with different kinds of people. If you work at making a difference in a safe environment, this skill will come more easily to you in a stressful situation.

Stumbling Block 2: I'm too old, weak, uncoordinated, short, or shy to be able to defend myself effectively.

If a man is much larger than you are, trained as a fighter, *and* expects resistance from you, you will have a hard time defending yourself physically. But the chances of all three of those elements being met are fairly slim. Although you have no control over your size, the size of the attacker, or the training he might have, you do have a lot of control over his expectations.

Particularly if you are small, you have a tremendous advantage because the last thing he will expect is resistance. Your resistance does not even have to be physical. Because a rapist is most interested in control and power, if you are not intimidated by him, you have taken a big first step toward thwarting an attack.

As long as you can keep your wits about you, you will not be defenseless, no matter how old, unathletic, uncoordinated, or how small you are. Your best weapon is your brain. Use it.

There are many stories about elderly women who were attacked and were able to defend themselves successfully. Age has nothing to do with self-defense.

If you can't outmuscle him, you've got to outmaneuver him. Even if you are not by nature a loud and obnoxious person, you need to make sure that you are capable of overcoming your shyness long enough to shout, cause a scene, and escape to safety.

Stumbling Block 3: I can't scream. I just wasn't raised that way.

Many women are truly convinced that they could not scream if they wanted to. Perhaps the key word here is *wanted*. If you had to, it might be easier. Although it might be contrary to the way you were raised or to your image of a "respectable lady" or a "good girl," when you are faced with the question of your own survival, you need to put these stereotyped self-images out of mind. Just because you scream and holler and kick and fight to save your life, it does not mean that you have turned into a barroom brawler.

To set your mind at ease that you *can* scream if necessary, practice yelling and speaking assertively.

Make sure you put forth a strong yell instead of a high-pitched scream. You want to sound forceful, not panic striken. Besides, you can damage your vocal cords if you scream, whereas a good, loud yell won't hurt you.

Stumbling Block 4: I can't get angry.

If you are ever attacked, the most natural response in the world is fear, followed by anger. When you express your anger, you will be able to defend yourself much more effectively than if you remain scared.

Many women never show their anger. Keeping these emotions bottled up inside is not healthy physically or psychologically. If you never allow yourself to show your anger, it will be hard for you to get mad when you need to.

If getting angry is not something that comes to you naturally, you might need to practice it. Go somewhere where you are safe and by yourself.

Imagine that you are being attacked, that some smelly guy off the street is pushing at you, trying to get you on the ground. How dare he! He has no right to do this! Suddenly you are no longer frightened. You are angry.

Pretend that you have turned to him, and begin to shout whatever comes to mind. It doesn't matter. The important thing is that you begin to release your anger.

Anger can be debilitating, or it can be helpful in a stressful and dangerous situation. Many law enforcement officers have told me that they use their anger. It gives them courage and strength.

Anger is only dangerous when it is uncontrolled. If you practice getting mad, you will learn how to use your anger safely and effectively.

One of the best illustrations of releasing built-up anger was shown in the wonderful 1992 movie *Fried Green Tomatoes*. The main character, Evelyn, was a slightly overweight, middle-aged woman who had tried all her life to "be good." When circumstances finally pushed her over the edge, she got mad. Really mad. Shouting her battle cry, "Towanda!" she changed from being shy and unassuming to being a strong, aggressive woman.

Stumbling Block 5: I feel guilty if I'm rude.

Trying to remain polite has resulted in more women being raped than perhaps any other single reason. If your date is getting heavy handed and you don't stop him because you don't want to be rude, you're putting yourself in danger.

If the man on the street asks you to take him to the nearest gas station because his car has stalled and you do it because you don't want to be rude, you're putting yourself in danger.

If your boss asks you to stay late and help him with a project after everyone else has gone home and you say yes to be nice, even though you heard that he raped his last secretary, you are putting yourself in danger.

There is no way for you to remain polite throughout your entire life. Your safety depends on your ability to say "no" when necessary and to be rude if need be.

If necessary, look at the potential attacker for a moment. Does he have *your* best interests in mind? Is he being thoughtful of the way *you* are feeling?

We must embrace a new etiquette if we are to learn to protect ourselves effectively. We must be assertive and on guard. We don't have to be rude and shout obscenities at anyone, but we are under no obligation to stop and give directions to a stranger either.

When a potential attacker meets with your assertive response, he probably will make you feel guilty about your attitude. He may respond by saying something like, "Hey, you don't have to be so mean to me. I only asked for the time of day." He may accuse you of being cold, paranoid, or crazy. So expect a rude, intimidating response. You may even be pleasantly surprised that it doesn't come, but you won't be caught off guard if it does.

Women respond to guilt and flattery too easily. Stay alert. Don't fall into a trap. Remember that you don't owe this guy on the street a thing. If you want to help the homeless, the poor, and the down-and-out, do it under the auspices of an organization that will offer you safety while you are offering help.

It is particularly difficult for some women to be rude to someone they know, no matter how casually. This is partly responsible for a tremendous number of acquaintance rapes.

It is also difficult for young girls to say "no" or to be rude to someone they know, especially if it is someone of authority. It is as important to teach our children to say "No!" as it is to say "Yes, sir." It is as important for them to say, "Leave me alone," as it is to say, "Please" and "Thank you."

Cultured manners are for refined, civilized situations. Possible rape is not civilized; it calls for a different kind of behavior.

Survival is more important than being polite.

"Although a receptive and approachable woman helps make relationships and homes warm, taking these same qualities out into the world can lead to uninvited intrusions."—Jean Shinoda Bolen, *The Goddess in Everywoman*

Stumbling Block 6: I don't want to appear foolish.

Sometimes we get so caught up in the moment that we find it difficult to keep our perspective. One of the most ridiculous examples of this involves a vase of flowers, a car, and myself.

A couple of years ago I was assigned the task of arranging flowers for a party that several friends and I were giving. I fussed and fumed and fixed for hours, trying to get the flowers just right. The result was a respectable arrangement.

Driving to the party, I had the flowers carefully perched on the front seat beside me. Suddenly a car pulled out in front of me. For just a split second I hesitated, thinking, if I swerved my flowers would fall over and be ruined. Fortunately, my common sense took over and I did swerve, avoiding the car. The flowers were ruined. I was disappointed, of course, but the alternative was unthinkable.

If you stop and think, Which is more important, your life or a vase of flowers? it is laughable. And yet, many of us lose sight of the big picture. Put yourself into another situation.

Suppose you are at a fraternity house with a boy, and he starts to threaten you and make heavy advances. Your alternatives? Scream for help and appear a little foolish, or be raped with the possibility of contracting AIDs or becoming pregnant.

Or imagine yourself in the lobby of a large, old building waiting for the elevator. When one finally comes, you start to get on but the only other person on the elevator is a young, strong, tough looking guy who definitely makes you nervous. Your alternatives? You could go ahead and get on the elevator, taking your chances on being raped, assaulted, or robbed, so you won't hurt his feelings. Or you could appear a little foolish or paranoid—but safe—and quietly wait for the next elevator.

When presented in black and white, the choices are so clear it is ridiculous. Consider the following examples.
Would you rather:

1. Look ridiculous by crawling out of the bathroom window to safety . . . or keep your "dignity" by allowing yourself to be raped at a party?
2. Appear paranoid because you went to a neighbor's house rather than drive home because someone was following you . . . or appear brave and have the man follow you to the garage and rape you before you made it into the house?
3. Look like a real baby by calling your dad to come get you . . . or allow a drunk and pushy date to drive you home and be sexually assaulted on the way?
4. Refuse to let him in and be ridiculed by the man at the door who says he has a package and needs your signature . . . or let him in only to find out that there is no package and the police are after him for multiple rapes?

Stumbling Block 7: I would never be able to hurt someone.

This is a tough one. Women are nurturing, caring, loving individuals. It is difficult for us to contemplate purposefully inflicting pain on someone else, so this is an issue that you need to deal with now, *before* something happens to you. The question is, Would you be able to use your strength and skills to hurt someone to save your life or to keep you from being raped?

No one can answer this for you. This is a deeply personal question. It may be helpful to remember a few things about being attacked, however, while you are making this decision.

When someone attacks you with the intent to harm you, they have given up their right to fair play. No one has the right to harm you in any way, whether by threatening you verbally, bullying you into doing something you do not want to do, or causing you physical or mental pain.

Suppose you are hurrying to your car late one afternoon. Almost everyone has already left to go home, and the street is pretty much deserted. You're tired and anxious to get home, and you don't even notice the man crouched between your car and the next one.

He jumps out at you and pulls you toward him before you realize what is happening. You are terrified, of course, and then very, very angry. He starts to pull at your clothes, his face close to yours. You remember from your self-defense training that if you strike him in the eyes it will hurt so much he will probably let you go immediately. Can you do it? Yes! He doesn't care about you! Why should you care about him? This is not a polite game of tennis where he serves first and then allows you to serve. He's going to keep complete control of the game until you fight for your rights.

How Much Force Can You Use?

You have the right to fight to defend yourself. You have the right to do whatever is necessary to keep yourself safe. In defending yourself, you are allowed by law to use as much force against an attacker as is used—or threatened—against you.

If an attacker walks up to you, calls you a dirty name, and asks you to go out one night, you do not have the right to swing around, break his jaw, and dislocate his knee. This is excessive force for the amount of danger you faced.

However, if a man walks up to you, grabs you around the neck, and starts choking you, you can use whatever means you have available to save yourself. This is a life-threatening situation.

IN A NUTSHELL

1. Women are stronger, faster, smarter, and more powerful than we give ourselves credit for being.
2. Emphasize what you can do to keep yourself safe rather than worrying about things that you cannot do.
3. If you use your wits and use the strength and power that is within you, you can defend yourself effectively.
4. Just because you cause a scene to defend yourself does not mean that you have lost your good manners. Manners have nothing to do with survival.
5. You *can* make a difference. You must use your knowledge and skills to keep safe.
6. If you are attacked, the most natural response is fear, followed by anger. It's OK to get angry.
7. You are not responsible for the good will of everyone you meet.
8. It is better to look a little foolish than to be raped.
9. Don't get caught up in the moment. Make choices based on the big picture.
10. If someone attacks you, he has given up his right to fair play.
11. You have the right to fight to defend yourself.

Exercises 1 and 2 allow you to feel powerful and to realize your strength, both physically and verbally. For more physical exercises, see chapter 10; and for stronger communication skills, see chapter 5.

Exercise 3 allows you to practice venting your anger in a safe environment.

Exercise 1

Feeling the power within.

No matter how small, thin, or delicate you may think you are, you still have the potential to exert tremendous power. None of us uses our full physical potential. If you think you aren't very strong, try this exercise to prove to yourself that you are powerful (it's also a great way to release tension and anger).

Get a plastic baseball bat at a toy store. Place an open slick magazine (any kind will do, but one of the girlie magazines is my first choice) on a bed. Take the bat and just beat the tar out of the magazine. You'll be astounded at the tremendous "thwack" that the bat makes. This has the advantage of *sounding* powerful as well as being potent.

Exercise 2

If you are embarrassed to practice yelling, go to the bathroom and turn on the tap full force. With the vent fan going and the water roaring, no one will be able to hear you. Go ahead and yell. Start by saying "No!" and build up to anything you want to say forcefully. Things like, "Get your hands off of me!" and "Leave me alone——" are popular choices. Or just yell as loudly as you can.

Exercise 3

A safe way to express anger.

Try shutting yourself up in a safe room all by yourself. This could be your bedroom, the bathroom, or the laundry room where you have the safety of the tumble and roar of the washer and dryer.

Begin by stating who and what you are angry about. Choose some inanimate object as that person and address it directly. For instance, choose a pillow to be your husband and let him have it.

Say, "I am so furious with you for being more interested in the ball game than the nice dinner I fixed for you. I spent all afternoon cooking, and I expected a little appreciation and some extra attention from you."

Then say what you want. "I want you to hug me and kiss me and tell me that I'm a good cook and that you can't believe all that I accomplish in one day. I want you to tell me that you could never run a household and that you really admire the way that I get things done."

If you can, get a friend to do a little role playing with you. Let her be the husband (or boyfriend or whoever). Then get her to tell you exactly what you would like to hear from your husband or boyfriend. It's play acting, but it is effective.

The most effective means of all is to sit down with your husband or boyfriend and tell him honestly that this is how you feel. Wait until you feel you can control your anger, but be honest. You're taking a risk, because you are changing the roles and asserting yourself and showing honest feelings, but the other risk is in continuing to keep your anger bottled up inside.

4

Building Self-esteem and Becoming Assertive

Robin hurried down the street, glancing nervously behind her. All she could think of was her mother's warning, "Don't be too late. I don't want you downtown by yourself after dark."

For once Robin wished she had listened to her mother.

As she rounded the corner, she walked a little faster. The subway stop was still two blocks away, and it was nearly dark already.

Suddenly a man stepped out of the alley in front of her, blocking her way. He held out his hand. "Can you spare some change? I'm out of work and have two hungry kids at home." Robin hesitated. He did look hungry, and she hated the thought of hungry kids.

At her hesitation, the man moved closer. Robin saw a look in his eye that she did not like at all. "Come on, girl, you'd feed a couple of kids, wouldn't you?" and he reached out as if to grab her arm.

It was enough for Robin. She stood up straighter and spoke loudly, "If you want help for your kids, go to the St. Luke's shelter tonight. They'll help you."

The man's expression became menacing. "I bet you've got enough on you to feed us for a week. What kind of girl are you, letting two little kids go hungry?"

But Robin was not going to be intimidated. She began walking again and crossed the street. "If you don't leave me alone this instant, I'm going to yell for the police. And anyway, if you're so worried about your kids, you should be home looking after them."

Robin walked quickly to the corner and into the first store she saw open. The man called after her, cursing her for being cold-hearted and cruel, but Robin closed her ears to his abuse, knowing that she was only smart, not cruel.

The Importance of Self-esteem

One of the facts most basic to self-defense is that you have to believe you are worth defending. Many women are so wracked with doubts about themselves and have such low self-images, they resign themselves to whatever fate brings them.

This is particularly true when rape is involved. Rape is the only crime where the victim is made to feel guilty, and guilt is a big stumbling block to building a good self-image. Feeling guilty is so common among rape victims that many women do not tell anyone when they have been raped, and many more refuse to report the crime to the authorities.

Building a good self-image is critical to living your life without fear. Yet it is fear that keeps many of us from believing in ourselves. We fear we will fail, and then we fear that if we do fail, we will be rejected by the ones we love.

Self-esteem is a recognition and appreciation of who you are, separate from who your fmaily is, what your profession is, or what kind of house you live in.

Think of your self-esteem as a bank account. You will make deposits or withdrawals based on your actions. For instance, if you go out drinking with a group of girls on Friday night and leave your baby sister home alone, that's a pretty rotten thing to do. You have taken a big withdrawal out of your self-esteem bank.

On the other hand, if you gave up a date to go to a concert and stayed home with your best friend who just broke up with her boyfriend and really needed to talk to you, then you've made a handsome deposit to your self-esteem.

People gain self-esteem in different ways. To some, the most important thing in the world is to be trusted. For them, being deserving of the loving trust of a friend is what makes them feel good about themselves.

Another person may feel that being needed is of utmost importance. A mother caring for a young infant is filled with self-esteem because she knows that the child needs her and she is able to fill this need.

Living life with honesty and integrity also can help build self-esteem. If we can remain honest, even when lying would *seem* to get us out of difficulty, and maintain our integrity in the face of great temptations, then we add to our bank of self-esteem.

Actually, the rules are very simple. You add to your self-esteem account by doing those things that are full of integrity and make you feel proud of yourself. We can be proud of our creativity, our self-discipline, our perseverance, or our skills. The important thing is that we recognize the good in ourselves and feel pride in our accomplishments.

Withdrawals happen when we cheat ourselves or others, or ignoring the maxims of honesty, loyalty, trust, and honor.

The dividends? George Gallup conducted a poll on the self-esteem of the American public. His findings indicated that people with high self-esteem led fuller, richer lives. They had a strong sense of family and a high degree of success with interpersonal relationships. They were more productive and less prone to chemical addictions, and they were more generous with their time and money, giving to charitable causes and community activities.

Steps to Building Self-esteem

1. Get to know yourself. You can do this either by yourself or with the help of a close friend or family member. Get out a pencil and piece of paper, and divide the paper into two columns. At the top of one side write Good Things and on the top of the other write Not-so-good Things. Then do an honest apprasial of yourself.

Under the first column, you might list the things that you really like about yourself. Are you creative? honest? loving? cheerful? List them all! You should be proud of your good characteristics.

Be equally as honest in listing your not-so-good characteristics. Under this column you might list short-tempered, lazy, or whatever characteristics you feel need work.

Now write a short paragraph describing the ideal you. If you can imagine it, you can attain it.

2. Forgive yourself—realize that we all make mistakes. No one is perfect. Be kind to yourself, and forgive your imperfections.

One of my favorite stories is of two monks traveling together. When they came to a river, a beautiful woman was standing by the water. The older monk offered to carry her across, and she accepted gratefully. At the far side of the river, he put her down and they continued their journey.

After several miles, the younger monk could contain himself no longer. "Brother, how could you carry that woman across the water after you took a vow never to touch a woman?"

The older monk turned to him. "I left the woman at the edge of the river. It seems that you are carrying her still."

Know when to let go. Don't keep carrying your mistakes with you.

If you tend to berate yourself over your imperfections, try this. Keep a pad and pencil by your bed. At the end of the day, write, "I forgive myself for" and continue with anything that comes to mind. Did you yell at the kids? Did you goof off instead of studying for exams? Did you hang up on your mother? You deserve forgiveness for whatever you did. Use each mistake as a learning experience.

3. *Be kind to yourself.* Treat yourself as you would one of your children or your best friend. Know that bad things do happen to good people for no apparent reason. When life gets tough, be sweet and gentle with yourself and ride out the storm.

If things get really rough, treat yourself to some of life's little pleasures. Sleep late one morning. Buy yourself some flowers at the market. Take a warm bubble bath, and read a good book. If you treat yourself like someone worthy of love and attention, you'll soon begin to feel like someone worthy of love and attention.

4. *Challenge yourself.* Learn to confront and resolve difficulties. For most of us, it is easier to avoid confrontation than it is to resolve it. This is true of problems at work, with relationships or with our own personal growth. Imagine that you and your mother argue every time you are together. It doesn't seem to matter what you are talking about, you just get on each other's nerves.

If you are determined to stop arguing, you have two options: You can avoid your mother, or you can try to figure out why you argue and work at the root of the problem. Option one is easier, but it would be sad to have to avoid your mother the rest of her (or your) life. Option two is a great deal more difficult, but the rewards are also much greater. By discovering why you and your mother argue, you have opened up avenues for growth for both of you. In confronting and resolving your problem in this way, you have made a major investment in your self-esteem.

5. *Believe in yourself.* Everyone likes to have the love and support of friends and loved ones. But remember that you came into this world all by yourself, and in the end you will leave all by yourself. You are whole unto yourself. You do not have to have anyone else to make your life complete.

Luckily, there probably are people in your life who will stand by you no matter what you do. So many times we are afraid to admit our mistakes because we are afraid that we will lose the love and respect of those that we are closest to. If these people truly deserve our love, then they will stick by us and will be there for us no matter what kind of mistakes we might make. Unconditional love is one of life's most precious treasures.

To prove your belief in yourself, make a list of the things you can trust yourself to do. Start with the simple: I trust myself to get to class on time or to work on time. I trust myself to take care of my body.

Then you might move on to some more general, philosophical statements: I trust myself to raise my children in the best way I know how. I trust myself to adhere to a personal code of honor, trust, and integrity.

Whatever you trust yourself to do, write it down. With a list in front of you, it's easier to say, "Yes, I really am trustworthy. I can believe in myself."

By believing in yourself and in the love of those closest to you, you can overcome your fear of abandonment and grow into the woman you want to be.

6. *Accept and love yourself.* If you know and believe in yourself and forgive yourself for your mistakes, you can begin to accept and love yourself. Work hard to change the things you like least about yourself, but know there are some things about yourself you cannot change.

For instance, our age, race, and basic physical makeup are unalterable. We may not like the fact that we are forty, fifty, or sixty years old, but if we are, we are. We may not like it that we are short, have big feet, or bulging eyes, but these too are impossible to change. What we do have control over is how we deal with increasing age or with certain physical defects. If we spend our days moaning about getting old, we have wasted time and energy and have taken a big withdrawal from our self-esteem account. Learn to live with yourself. Accept the mundane, and love the divine.

6. *Go beyond yourself.* Building self-esteem is a liberating experience, for it releases us from the cloying need to worry and fret about who we are and what we are about. Armed with a healthy self-esteem, we can assertively and lovingly take care of

ourselves and of others whom we love.

With a rich account of self-esteem, we can afford to give to others. The dividends will multiply rapidly.

Assertive Women

A critical part of successful self-defense comes from being a strong, assertive woman. But assertiveness needs to be built on a healthy self-esteem. People who are assertive but do not have respect for themselves usually end up being arrogant, pushy, and haughty. Only people who believe in themselves and their worth as individuals are able to use assertiveness with skill and grace.

My ideal of an assertive woman is a friend I've known for several years. Wendy is in no way masculine looking; she's simply a strong woman. I like the way she stands—feet slightly apart, arms comfortably hanging by her sides, head tilted forward a little as if she wants to catch every word you say. Though calm and gentle, this woman is so self-assured she is steadfast in times of crisis. She knows what she believes in, is conscious of and accepts her own shortcomings, and is proud of what she does and who she is. I am proud to call her a friend, and I seek her out when I am troubled.

Being assertive is different from being angry and rude. It simply means being positive, strong-willed, and confident enough of your basic rights to stand firm on any issue.

Manuel J. Smith writes in his book *When I Say No I Feel Guilty* that all of us share certain basic rights.

- You have the right to be independent of the good will of others.
- You have the right to say, "I don't care."
- You have the right to please yourself before you please others.
- You have the right to like yourself even if others appear not to.

Assertiveness and Relationships

These basic rights do not sit comfortably with many of us. They sound selfish and self-centered. But then, many of us have been taught from an early age to give up our own rights to make and keep peaceful relationships. We have been taught to be polite to *everyone,* to put others' needs and wants above our own.

Because relationships are so important to women, we have been taught not to alienate others. We make sure other people like us, even if we don't particularly like them.

We are nice to the foul-tempered clerk at the grocery store; we wave politely to the teenager who cuts in front of us in traffic; we listen politely—and interminably—to the telemarketer who has interrupted dinner for the third time this week.

Relationships are so important to us that sometimes we are guilty of being naive and trusting to a fault.

Forty-two percent of the women who were raped said they had sex again with the men who raped them.—*Ms.* magazine study on date rape

---

We All Want to Help

We used to be able to take someone off the street, give him a hot meal and work to do for a few days, and both of us would be richer for the experience. We cannot be so trusting and naive today. We must be wary, and we must be careful when dealing with people we do not know very well. *Although safety and kindness are not mutually exclusive, we must find ways to show kindness that do not put us in danger.*

A few years ago, an elderly couple in my neighborhood decided to help out a stranger who arrived on their doorstep asking for work. The man was in obvious need of help, so they gave him a shovel and told him that he could work in their garden for the day.

The man repaid their kindness by hitting the woman over the head with the shovel. He killed her and severely injured her husband.

Although this is an extreme example, such occurrences happen often enough to convince us that caution is necessary.

Once you have allowed a man inside your home, you have given him an isolated spot and an opportunity to commit a crime. If you allow the wrong people into your house, your home can change from a haven to a prison.

When someone arrives on your doorstep seeking entrance to your home, it sometimes takes an assertive attitude to turn him away. Do not let him bully you or intimidate you into opening the door. Uniforms and identification badges can look fairly official, but they also can be purchased at a costume store. You must believe in your own rights and in your right to say no; you must stick to these rights. You may feel a little foolish shouting through a closed door, but it is much better to feel foolish than to wish you had. (For more information about staying safe in your home, see chapter 11.)

Being Assertive with Figures of Authority

In becoming an assertive woman, you will acquire powers that you never knew you had before. By standing up for yourself in a variety of different circumstances, you will be able to deal more effectively with people and events, adding to your own personal safety.

An assertive attitude will help you at home, in school, and in the workplace. It may make it possible for you to deal effectively with circumstances that could have disastrous results otherwise.

For instance, suppose you are staying late at your job, trying to finish a proposal your boss needs the next day. As you are locking up the office, one of the senior officers of the company walks up and compliments you on your skirt, which happens to be very short. He takes a couple of steps closer to you, and you begin to feel distinctly uncomfortable. When he reaches out and takes your arm, he tells you he can help you get the promotion you've been wanting.

You can react in a variety of ways. You can: (a) scream, tell him to get his ——ing hands off you, kick him in the groin, and break his nose; (b) not say anything and go along with him; (c) firmly remove his hand, telling him not to touch you again and that sexual pressure is against company policy; (d) pull at his hand, crying and begging for him to leave you alone.

Choice *a* is overdoing it. It is simply a reaction without thought or consideration. You have not been threatened with great danger, and you have overreacted. Should his advances have escalated, you might have been justified in using this response, but not yet.

Choice *b* is the most dangerous. This could very well lead to rape in the back room. This is a "no action" response, where a woman pretends that this could not be happening to her or that it is inevitable and she couldn't do anything to prevent it.

Choice *d* is ineffective because he is on a power kick anyway. Otherwise, why would he try to use his position to get what he wanted? Pleading and begging will only add fuel to the fire. This choice indicates that you want the *favor* of being left alone, not that you are asserting the right to the privacy of your body.

The only logical choice under these particular circumstances is choice *c*. By communicating with him directly and telling him exactly what to do and not to do, you are showing that you believe in yourself and in your basic rights.

Confronting someone in a position of authority is very difficult for many of us, but it can be particularly intimidating—and dangerous—for young girls. Accustomed to trusting teachers or other adults, they find it difficult to recognize danger or the escalation of danger when it comes from an older person whom they trust.

Girls and boys should be taught at an early age to believe in themselves and to believe in what they know is right. Even practicing saying "No!" assertively will help a youngster become more confident.

Are You Assertive?

Assertiveness at any age is an essential tool for staying safe. Assertive people project an "I can take care of myself" kind of image. This attitude is exactly what a potential rapist is NOT looking for. Are you a power player? Do you:

- try not to hurt anyone's feelings?
- communicate indirectly so you won't offend anyone?
- hesitate to say what you are thinking, in case it's an incorrect or unpopular opinion?
- rarely end up saying what you mean?
- try to please as many people as possible as often as you can?
- avoid confrontation even if it means giving up your rights?

If you answered yes, consider these traits of powerful people. They:

- know that even when they are as fair and honest as possible, someone is going to have hurt feelings;
- communicate directly and honestly;
- are more concerned with achieving results than avoiding mistakes;
- say exactly what they mean to say;
- know that being true to their inner integrity is more important than trying to please people;
- know that confrontation is inevitable and that it can be a useful and stimulating point of growth.

What's so great about being powerful and assertive? Why should we try to develop these characteristics? Powerful people report that they:

- feel good about themselves;
- are more effective with people, more efficient with their time;
- don't have that nagging feeling that someone is always taking advantage of them;
- feel that they are not being overly naive and innocent;
- keep themselves out of dangerous situations by knowing how to say No!

> "I have more confidence than I do talent, and I think that confidence is the main achiever of success."—Dolly Parton

How assertive are you?

The next time you are with a group of women, try this test. Have each of you say your name, but don't tell anyone else what this is about. You will probably be amazed at how many of you say your name with a rising inflection at the end, as if you are asking a question. Go around again, this time with each of you saying your name with an air of confidence and self-assurance.

You are not born with assertiveness and power. These traits are not in any way unattainable for any of us. These are characteristics that can be learned and practiced until they become part of our basic nature. Learning to be powerful, honest, and assertive is a lot like learning any new skill. It takes time and effort, and you will invariably make mistakes while you are perfecting these skills.

At first you may make a few mistakes. You might be overly adamant about some things that really don't warrant that much attention, or your voice may squeak or falter when you tell someone how you believe about certain issues. You will feel guilty when someone says, "But you used to be so sweet!" and you'll wonder if all this assertiveness business is really worth it.

It is. Showing others that we believe in ourselves is the first step to building open, honest relationships.

In becoming assertive women, we are not trying to "be like a man." Instead, we are becoming strong women. This strength is an incomparable gift to ourselves and the finest legacy that we could possibly give our daughters.

Oliver Wendell Holmes said, "What lies behind us and what lies before us are tiny matters compared to what lies within us."

IN A NUTSHELL

1. To defend yourself successfully, you have to believe you are worth defending.
2. People with high self-esteem have better relationships, are more productive, are less prone to chemical addiction, and are more generous with their time and money.
3. Building self-esteem involves getting to know yourself, forgiving yourself, trusting, and loving yourself.
4. Although safety and kindness are not mutually exclusive, we must find ways to show kindness that do not put us in danger.
5. Recognizing danger from a figure of authority is often difficult, particularly for young people.
6. Assertiveness at any age is an essential trait for staying safe.
7. Being assertive is different from being angry and rude. Being assertive simply means being positive, strong-willed, and confident.
8. Acting assertively helps you deal with people more effectively and use time more efficiently.
9. Assertive people communicate directly and honestly, are more concerned with achieving results than avoiding mistakes, and know that confrontation is inevitable and can be a useful part of growth.
10. Believing in ourselves is the basis for acting assertively.
11. Showing others that we believe in ourselves is a first step to building open, honest relationships.

Note: Assertiveness training is a wonderfully empowering tool for anyone, whether a corporate executive, a teacher, or a mother. Many counselors offer one-day workshops or weekend training sessions. If you can, participate in one. It may be a life-changing experience for you.

There are many exercises you can also do on your own at home.

Exercise 1

Stephen R. Covey suggests in his best seller, *The Seven Habits of Highly Effective People,* that there are two ways we can put ourselves in control of our lives immediately:

We can make a promise and keep it;
We can set a goal and attain it.

He suggests that "as we begin to make and keep commitments, even small commitments, we begin to establish an inner integrity that gives us the awareness of self-control and the courage and strength to accept more of the responsibility for our own lives."

This is an excellent resource book. Highly recommended.

Exercise 2

Many women suffer from a lack of self-esteem because they feel as if they have no control over their lives. Events and actions sweep over them, making them spin in a tidal wave of life.

Many activities will help you feel more "in tune" with the world and less dependent on those around you. These will help you feel more in control of your life:

- Keep track of where your money goes. For at least one month, write down everything you spend.
- Read the newspaper every day for a week. Don't depend on anyone else to tell you what is going on in the world. Keeping informed is a responsibility of all mature adults.
- Balance your own checkbook.
- Plan an evening for you and your favorite person. You make the reservations and arrange for transportation.

Exercise 3

Get rid of those wishy-washy feelings.

Get a stack of wooden popsicle sticks. On each list one of your characteristics you dislike that keep you from being assertive. These may be general things, such as you can't say no or you avoid confrontations; or they may be specific, such as "I can't tell Joe that he drives me crazy when he sings" or "I keep telling the program chairman that I'll do it when I really don't want to." Whatever characteristics you want to get rid of, write them down.

Take the sticks and glue them together in some sort of structure. After you are finished and the glue has dried, do away with the structure in any way that seems appropriate to you. You might throw it off a bridge, crush it under the tires of your car, burn it, or smash it with your fist. Getting rid of it will be a wonderfully liberating experience. It will give you renewed energy in building self-esteem.

Exercise 4

Practice looking cocky. Throw your chin into the air like a queen. Swagger like a sailor. Walk as if you owned the world. Try a little play acting and portray each of these characters:

- The bionic woman—you're invulnerable and incredibly strong
- The Queen of Hearts in *Alice in Wonderland*
- Thelma and Louise from the movie *Thelma and Louise*
- Superman, only this time it is Superwoman!

5

Acquaintance and Date Rape

Jim was the most exciting man Lisa had ever met. Good looking and from a wealthy family, he was the kind of guy she had always dreamed of marrying. They had been going out for a month, and already Lisa had plans—big plans. She found Jim touchingly attentive and she liked that; it made her feel loved. He insisted on taking care of her totally when they went out, opening doors for her, choosing where they would go and when. He did have a nasty temper and was sometimes irrationally jealous, but she was sure that would change.

When he picked her up from the dorm on Friday, he greeted her happily, "Hey, guess what? Mother and Dad are out of town, and we get the big house all to ourselves. Look! Champagne to celebrate."

Lisa laughed delightedly. "Are we supposed to drink all of that in one night?" she asked, still laughing but a little puzzled. Jim knew she didn't drink.

Jim grinned back. "Well, you never know what's going to happen."

Something in his tone checked Lisa's laughter. It wasn't sinister, exactly. It just made her uncomfortable.

Jim opened the car door for her. "I didn't see you talking with Frank this afternoon, did I?"

Lisa's heart sank, and she tried to look casual, afraid that the afternoon would be spoiled. "It was nothing, Jim. He was just asking about the English paper."

Jim slammed the door and stormed around the car. "I told you! I told you not to mess with him anymore. Why don't you do what I ask? Is it too much to ask?"

Tears welled up in Lisa's eyes. "I'm sorry, Jim. I didn't think you would mind." Her voice was low.

Jim remained in a stormy mood the rest of the afternoon. As soon as they got to his parent's house in the suburbs, Jim started drinking. Lisa wandered around the house, dreaming about the day that she would belong here. She kept a wary eye out for Jim, but he seemed involved in watching the ball game on television.

Suddenly she had an idea. Maybe she could draw Jim out of his mood by kissing him or something. She swallowed nervously. She came from a small town, and her parents had never allowed her to go out much. She wasn't sure how much she was supposed to do on a date because she had always let Jim take the lead.

As she came up behind him, Jim did not even turn to acknowledge her presence. Shaking a little, she slipped her arms around his shoulders and kissed his ear. He whirled and grabbed her arms, pulling her over the sofa.

"Trying to make it up to me, huh, kitten?" his words were slurred. He kissed her roughly. Lisa gasped with surprise. Suddenly he was pushing her into the sofa, his hands grabbing at her breasts. She struggled against him.

"Where are you going? You're the one that started this. Guess you'll finish it too."

Lisa stared at him, her heart pounding. What was he talking about? He couldn't really think that she wanted to have sex! And suddenly she was scared. "Please, Jim. Stop! Please stop."

Jim held her down with the weight of his body and began pulling at her clothes. Suddenly hot, blazing anger consumed her. She screamed, and the sound of it scared her. Jim clamped a hand over her mouth.

"What are you doing? What if someone hears you? They'd think I was raping you or something."

Lisa turned until he released her mouth. In a voice quivering with anger she shouted, "It is rape. Now get the hell off me, or I'm screaming until everybody in the neighborhood hears me."

Jim got up, smoothing down his clothes. "Get out of here!" he shouted. "You'll never live in a house like this."

Lisa grabbed her things and ran out the door, sure that she never wanted to live in a house like that.

Whom Can I Trust?

To a young woman, the thought of date rape may be the most frightening aspect of moving out on her own. The delightful anticipation of freedom is all too often grounded with a heavy sense of dread. The joy of going to college or beginning the first job and moving into an apartment for the first time is touched with the reality of the threat of rape.

> One out of every eight women has been raped, and 80 percent of these have been committed by acquaintances.

All women are aware of the problem, and our response to it varies from having a vague sense of uneasiness to outright paranoia about our safety. The media have overwhelmed us with scandals and stories of date rape. It is a subject that holds a horrifying fascination for us, for it occurs with unbelievable frequency. According to the National Victim Center, one out of every eight women have been raped and 80 percent of these rapes have been committed by acquaintances.

The situation in colleges and universities is even more startling, for one out of every four women in college in the United States has been the victim of rape or attempted rape.

In simple terms, acquaintance rape is rape by someone you have met previously. He may be someone you work with or someone you pick up at a bar or a party. He may be someone introduced to you through a friend or someone you met in a class.

Date rape is a bit more specific than this, for it is rape by someone you have willingly chosen to be with and have agreed to go out with. It may even be someone to whom you are attracted; otherwise you would not be interested in going out with him. Like Lisa, you may enjoy the man very much and even dream of a future with him.

Women are drawn to men for thousands of different reasons. Money, position, fame, physical looks are all elements that may play a role in whom we are attracted to. The media are full of stories of women who were so attracted to wealth or fame that they made serious judgmental errors. One of the more publicized ones resulted in the rape trial and conviction of the prize fighter Mike Tyson.

Sometimes it is the very element of danger in a man that we find attractive. For many women there is a certain primitive appeal of an aggressive, possessive guy. He is the kind of person who can make you feel momentarily safe against the world.

But safe from him as well? His personality should be handled with extreme caution, with safety foremost in your thoughts. Never, never take a chance with a man like this.

Acquaintance or date rapists don't wear badges identifying themselves as such. For the most part, they are guys who look just like regular guys.

Although there are no clear guidelines for identifying a man as a potential rapist, there are personality characteristics that indicate potential trouble. Most of these characteristics deal with issues of power and control. This is not to say that if a man opens your car door he will rape you, but each of the characteristics listed below should raise a red flag in your mind. The more of these characteristics that your potential date displays, the greater the distance you should put between the two of you.

☆ Red Flag Traits—characteristics of an acquaintance rapist

- He must control every situation—where you go, what you eat, what you wear, whom you see.
- He wants to be alone with you, isolating you from friends or other acquaintances.
- He has a cruel streak—verbal or physical.
- He is irrationally jealous.
- He gets angry if you try to pay for your own meal, drive yourself, plan activities.
- He abuses alcohol or drugs or insists that you do the same. He makes you feel naive and foolish if you don't.
- He views women as the "weaker sex" and thinks that they only exist to make his life pleasant for him.
- He insists that you wait on him hand and foot and makes you feel guilty if you don't.
- He demands your undivided attention, even when inappropriate, such as in a class.
- He is emotionally unstable, unable to control frustration or anger.
- He has a fascination with power (obsession with weapons, addiction to pornography).
- He acts overly friendly or familiar—treating you as if he knows you better than he does.
- He ignores your personal space—sits too close to you, puts his hands where and when you wish he wouldn't (on your knee, thigh, and so forth).

Find Out How He Would React

If you are unsure about your impending date, create a situation that will test him for some of the characteristics of an acquaintance rapist. If he overreacts or gets aggressively angry at any of these, be very careful.

- Test how controlling he is by:
  - suggesting that you plan the evening's activities;
  - suggesting that you drive and pick him up.

- Test his tendency to isolate you from friends by:
  - suggesting that you double-date with friends of yours.
- Test his attitude toward alcohol and drugs by:
  - telling him that you don't drink or do drugs.
- Test his *real* knowledge of you by:
  - telling him something you made up about yourself, like "I'm really a very shy person."
- Test his attitude toward woman by:
  - telling him about your brother-in-law who stays home with the kids every day while his wife goes to work.
- Test his tendency toward jealousy by:
  - telling him you got a letter from an old boyfriend.
- Test his attraction to power by:
  - asking his opinion on gun laws.
- Test his frustration level by:
  - making him wait fifteen minutes when he picks you up.
- Test his respect for your personal space by:
  - leaving an extra distance between you and him when you sit or stand together.

If you plan to go out with someone you don't know very well, watch him around others and listen to what he says to you, verbally and physically. Often a man will determine that he "is going to get some" and then will find a victim. He may approach you and actually give *you* a test before he asks you out.

He may give you little errands to do or ask you to wear a particular dress or fix your hair a certain way. How you react to his "test" may determine how he continues. If he puts his hand on your thigh or buttocks and you don't do anything, he may take you for an easy target. Remember that he may be reading your reactions as closely as you are reading his. If you don't want physical, sexual contact, make it perfectly clear from the very beginning.

If you decide to go out with him, keep your guard up until you get to know him well. Only meet in public places, and keep finding out more about his reactions. A little role reversal may unearth some surprising reactions. See what he does if:

- you order for him at the restaurant;
- you choose the wine for dinner;

- you open the doors for him;
- you choose the movie, buy the popcorn, and decide where you will sit.

Be Careful of Escalating Danger

Usually, if you are going to have trouble with an acquaintance or a date, the situation will gradually change from one of pleasant, or at least neutral, circumstances to one of great danger.

Andrea Parrot, an expert on acquaintance rape from Cornell University, has identified five different stages of an acquaintance rape that involves force or the threat of force:

1. A violation of a victim's personal space. (He sits too close, dances too close, keeps a hand on you at all times, puts his arm around your shoulders, puts a hand on your leg.)
2. The victim does not assert herself, does not tell the man that she doesn't like him sitting so close, putting his hands on her, and so forth. (She may not want to disturb the peace. She may just hope that nothing worse will happen. She's not sure that it *is* a sign of danger and may hesitate to say something. She may like this much physical contact.)
3. The assailant escalates the level of violation. For instance, he moves his hands from her thigh to her buttocks or breasts. (He's still testing, waiting for her reaction. If she still doesn't say anything, he may think he has it made. At this juncture he begins to get very aroused.)
4. The couple ends up in a secluded, vulnerable place. (He may make up some story or excuse for leaving a public place and going where they would be alone. Often he will tell his date that they are meeting friends or that his parents are home. She may be in a state of denial and may still be trying to pretend that the date is going well. She may be scared not to go along. She may be stoned or intoxicated and may be too lethargic to make a rational decision, or feeling too tired to insist on anything.)
5. The actual rape occurs.

✻   ✻   ✻

Not every date rape follows this order of events, of course, but enough do so that you should watch for some of these warning signs in your date and *in yourself.* Is he staying too close to you physically? Does he keep putting his hands all over you? If this makes you feel uncomfortable, are you able to tell him?

You've got to watch out for your own reactions as well as his. If your date makes you feel uncomfortable for any reason and you have a hard time telling him, you are quickly getting in over your head. *Now* is the time to bail out. Don't trust yourself and your ability to control him later on. If you can't tell him to get his hand off your knee, imagine how difficult it will be for you to assert yourself enough to make him get his naked body off of yours.

There are a lot of reasons why you might feel timid about asserting yourself with your date. Perhaps you haven't had a date in months and don't want to blow it. Perhaps you are trying to fit in. Perhaps you don't want to appear foolish.

Whatever the reason, for your own safety it is essential that you remain aware and alert to danger at any level. It is much easier to tell a man "Leave me alone!" when he's groping for your breasts than it is to poke him in the eye if he is attempting to rape you.

Don't be naive and overly trusting. Unless you know your date well and under a variey of situations, keep your guard up.

Lucy had known Brad in high school. He was a year older and had always treated her like a kid sister. When she saw him on campus soon after she arrived at college, she was thrilled when he asked her to a party on Friday. She even called her mother and told her she was going out with him and not to worry because she had known him in high school. Her mother was reassured.

When Brad picked her up Friday, he told her the party was at the lake house ten miles north of town. Lucy felt a twinge of misgiving but quickly squelched it when he teased, "You're not afraid to go with an old hometown boy, are you?" He pulled her close and kissed her. Lucy laughed, delighted with the attention. All the way to the lake, he made her sit right next to him.

When they arrived at the "party," no one else was at the house. Brad merely shrugged his shoulders and said he was sure everyone else was on the way. They started drinking almost immediately, and Brad began to get physical. By this time, Lucy was scared and asked to be taken home. Brad just laughed and started pulling at her jeans. Lucy clutched at her clothes and whimpered, "Please don't, Brad. Please just take me home."

When Brad told her to shut up and slapped her across the face, Lucy got hysterical. She screamed and cried, but Brad merely threatened to hit her again. Then he raped her.

When he finally took her back to campus, Lucy ran to the nearest phone and, sobbing, told her mother what had happened. Her mother came immediately and took her home. Lucy begged her mother not to tell anyone. Brad's family was well respected in the community, and Lucy didn't think anyone would believe her. Grudgingly, her mother finally agreed.

Lucy was engulfed with guilt and helplessness. She tried to go back to college but after a few weeks gave it up and came home. She was lethargic and severely depressed. Two months after the rape. Lucy tried to kill herself with an overdose of sleeping pills.

Rape of any kind, whether by a stranger or someone you grew up with, will most likely change your life forever. According to the *Ms.* magazine study on date rape, 30 percent of the victims contemplated suicide after the incident.

Rape is a tragedy. You will feel guilty; you will feel dirty; and you will feel terribly betrayed, particularly if it was someone you knew and liked who raped you. What you have to keep telling yourself over and over again, though, is that there is no such thing as justifiable rape. No matter *what* you do, you do not deserve to be raped.

Rape on Campus

There are a multitude of reasons for the widespread occurrence of rape on our college campuses, a woeful combination of factors. Away from home for the first time and giddy with newly found independence, young women make judgmental errors that often end in tragedy.

True independence is not simply moving away from home for the first time or having your own car. Real independence is being able to rely on yourself—on your abilities and the worth of your own judgment.

When you move away from your parents, you are not moving away from a set of rules that govern your life; you are only replacing your parents' rules with your own. In most cases, your own rules will be better and more applicable to your life than your parents'.

No longer will they be there to say, "No, you can't go out with him because I don't like the way he looks, or acts." You are the only one that can make that judgment. Now it's up to you to say, "Should I go out with this guy? Does he make me feel nervous or uncomfortable? Would I ever feel scared to be with him?"

You can get advice from your parents, from friends, from many different people, but ultimately the choice is yours.

The most dangerous time for a woman on campus is when she arrives at college for the first time. Unfamiliar with the layout of the campus, trying desperately to fit in and appear sophisticated, these women often do not make smart choices as to where they go and whom they go with.

Alcohol and drugs also play an undeniably strong role in the occurrence of acquaintance rape. According to the *Ms.* magazine survey, *"about 75 percent of the men and at least 55 percent of the women involved in acquaintance rapes had been drinking or taking drugs just before the attack."*

Alcohol and drugs slow your reaction time. When intoxicated, it is more difficult for you to respond to the presence or escalation of danger. Drinking alcohol saps your strength and makes it difficult to communicate clearly.

The third factor often present in acquaintance rape is the availability of isolated locations where an attack can be completed—the opportunity. Cars, fraternity rooms, empty dorm rooms, and abandoned beaches are places of potential danger if you are with the wrong man.

Very often a man will drive himself and his victim to an isolated spot. She may have romantic notions for a long, quiet walk on the beach or a sweet intimate talk while looking at the stars. He may be intent on getting her to a secluded spot so he can rape her. He likes having control over the transportation, and if he drives, the woman is dependent on him to get her home.

A tragic combination: the intent to rape, an isolated spot, and the use of alcohol or drugs.

Education and Communication

The idea of date rape is foreign to many men, even those who are guilty of the crime themselves. According to the *Ms.* study, 84 percent of men who had committed rape said what they did definitely was not rape.

One of the major problems with date rape is that so many men do not understand that it is rape. They have been taught to believe that sex is a game of conquest, that if they get lucky they will "score." To many men, a little resistance only adds to the fun. They like to tell themselves that when she says "no" she is only playing hard to get. She must really mean "yes."

Communicate clearly and effectively with your date. Set limits before passion sweeps either of you away. Say exactly what you mean. If you say "no," make sure you say it with conviction. If he continues to assault you, tell him you consider it rape.

If a woman says no to sex at any point, she has a right to be believed. If a man continues to force her, he is committing a crime; he is attempting to rape her.

There is no such thing as "justifiable rape." There are many myths that try to refute that. One of the most popular is that boys and men are unable to control themselves if they get worked up. This is the old idea of "blue balls." Another is that if a woman sexually teases a man, she deserves to be raped.

No one deserves to be raped. Every person is responsible for controlling himself or herself, no matter how passionate, angry, or frustrated he or she may become.

Although the victim should never be blamed in the case of acquaintance rape, there are things that we can do to lessen the chances of becoming a rape victim.

☆ If you do not know your date very well, or you have reason to be nervous or scared around him:

- Only meet him in safe, public places; avoid isolated places.
- Either drive yourself, or somehow provide your own transportation to and from the date.
- Dress appropriately. Get an idea of what others will be wearing, and go along with it until you trust your date.
- Don't abuse alcohol or drugs. Until you feel perfectly safe with this person, you will need all your senses. Don't dull them by drinking.
- Listen to your "inner voice." If you have a bad feeling about this date at any time, go home.
- Communicate with your date honestly and clearly. Tell him up front what you expect or what you don't expect.
- If at all possible, stay with a group of friends until you get to know your date a little better. There *is* safety in numbers.
- Do a little strategic planning before you go out. Make arrangements with someone to be on call if you need a ride home. At the very least, make sure you have enough money to call a cab. Either know your telephone credit card number or carry enough change to make a phone call.
- Believe in yourself. Don't accept a date with someone you don't need or want in your life. An evening at home by yourself is highly preferable to an evening with someone you don't like or who makes you feel uncomfortable.

A rape victim should never be blamed for being raped. Just as a woman who smokes cigarettes and spends her days basking in the sun does not *deserve* to get lung or skin cancer, her actions have increased her chances of doing so. None of us deserves to be raped, but we need to live responsibly to lessen this possibility.

From studies and surveys conducted with college men throughout the country, it is clear that some men take some actions as signals that a woman is willing to engage in sexual activities, even if this is not her intention. These actions include:

- dressing suggestively;
- agreeing to go back to his place;
- getting drunk or stoned;
- the woman asking the man out;
- the man paying for everything.

What Men Need to Know About Rape

A meaningful sexual relationship has to be built on respect for one other and consideration for what both persons want. If you want distinctly different things sexually, then it might be best to break up your relationship before either of you invests more time in it; for sex will always be a sore point between you.

If a man forces himself on a woman sexually against her wishes, it is rape, and rape is a criminal offense. A man may think that this is unfair; he may think that a woman deserves to be raped; he may think he is justified in forcing himself on her; but the law declares that if he has sexual intercourse with a woman against her will, he has committed rape. It doesn't matter what she was wearing, how many men she has been with, if she has aroused him, or even if she promised to have sex with him. She may have treated him unfairly and may have made some serious mistakes, but she still does not deserve to be raped. Men may disagree with this. They may fight this idea passionately, but the fact remains: rape is a criminal offense, and if you rape, you can be sent to jail for it.

The thought of going to jail is an undeniably strong deterrent for young men and a great incentive for them to restrain themselves sexually. Men can avoid trouble if they understand and follow a few basic guidelines:

- Never force a woman to have sex against her will. If she says she wants to stop, then stop. There is no way to justify losing control of your emotions and passions and forcing a woman.
- If a woman says no, assume that she means no.
- If you are getting mixed signals from a woman about what she wants sexually, stop and ask, then abide by her wishes. If she is pushing you farther than you want to go, let her know.
- Don't flatter yourself by believing that you know what a woman wants better than she knows herself, and don't buy into the old myth that sex is what she needs.

When There Is More Than One Attacker

Gang rape and party rape are also tragically common on college campuses. Often associated with fraternities or parties involving men's sports teams, these rapes occur when several men rape a woman. These rapes almost always involve alcohol and/or drugs. Such occurrences are often planned in advance, the men waiting for a victim and the opportunity.

The rules that are useful for avoiding rape by a single assailant are also useful, perhaps even more important, when there is more than one attacker. Do not allow yourself to be alone with several men. Stay with a girlfriend. If she has to leave a party early and there is no one else there whom you know, leave with her. Don't stay by yourself. If you suddenly find yourself isolated with a group of men who pose a threat to you, keep yourself in control. Don't become stoned or intoxicated in a strange place or situation, and leave as quickly as you can.

If you have to fight back physically, you will have a much tougher time than with a single assailant, particularly if your attackers are athletes.

But still know this: You are not helpless. Yell, cause a scene, and let them know in no uncertain terms that what they are doing is gang rape and against the law. Try to make eye contact with one of them, and tell him to go get help. If you can get at least one of them to humanize the situation, you might bring a little sanity to it.

"Between 1983 and 1986 football and basketball players representing NCAA-affiliated schools were reported to police for sexual assault approximately 38 percent more often than the average male on a college campus."—Rich Hofmann, sportswriter for the *Philadelphia Daily News*

It's Hard to Believe

It is more difficult to sense danger from a man you know than it is from a stranger on the street. Because we are lulled into a sense of safety with people we know, we usually are not as alert to danger and do not respond as strongly as the situation may call for.

The girl who was raped in a fraternity room—right next to a group of people who could have helped her—never raised her voice because she did not want to cause a scene. Another girl was raped by a boy who was not any larger than she was. She never fought back because she "didn't want to hurt him." Still another girl felt guilty and submitted to the rape when her date told her he simply could not control himself.

We are not responsible for the welfare of the men who rape us. Our first responsibility is to see to our own safety. These men are certainly not considering our needs and wants. Rape is an ugly, degrading crime, and rapists do not deserve our kindness or consideration.

IN A NUTSHELL

1. Acquaintance rape is rape by someone you have met previously.
2. It is often difficult to recognize danger from someone we know, particularly if it is a figure of authority such as an older relative or teacher.
3. Acquaintance rapists display certain general characteristics that can be recognized. Many of these characteristics deal with the issue of power and control.
4. Try to find out how a potential date will react under different circumstances before you go out with him.
5. Be aware of and respond to escalating danger—invasion of private space, increased physical contact, going to a secluded spot.
6. Men and women need to be educated about rape. Men should be aware that under any circumstance rape is a criminal offense.
7. There is no such thing as justifiable rape.
8. If you don't know your date very well, set some guidelines for yourself—meet only in public places, provide your own transportation, have someone you can call in an emergency, communicate with your date clearly and assertively.
9. Avoid situations where men might think it is all right to force sex on you, such as agreeing to go back to his place, getting drunk, allowing him to pay for everything, dressing revealingly.
10. Women on their own for the first time need to replace their parent's rules with their own.
11. Avoid drinking and taking drugs in new situations or with people you do not know well.
12. Be particularly cautious around groups of men, such as fraternities or college athlete parties.
13. Know that you have certain inviolable rights and that you can fight for these rights.

Note: It's a sad sign of our society that a woman has to practice before she goes out on a date, but a little planning may make the difference between the beginning of a wonderful relationship and the beginning of a nightmare.

Exercise 1

When a man asks you out and you are not sure whether or not you want to go, make a list of all the things you like about him and another list of any characteristics you do not like. Check the list on page 73 and see if any of these characteristics match.

I like _____

_____

_____

_____

_____

I don't like _____

_____

_____

_____

_____

Now ask yourself honestly: Is he aggressive? Demanding? Jealous? Is he sensitive to your feelings and what you want? Can you in any way imagine feeling scared around this man? Do you think you could trust him not to push you into a situation where you felt uncomfortable?

Exercise 2

Practice refusing a date. So many women accept dates they don't want just so they won't hurt someone's feelings. You can't take care of everybody in the world. When someone asks you out and you don't want to go for any reason, just say, "No thank you," and plan an evening out with the girls. This is hard for a lot of us. We have been programmed to believe that a date—any date—is preferable to sitting home alone.

Exercise 3

If you are contemplating going out with a man, sit down and do a best scenario and a worst scenario for the date. Make plans so that the worst scenario could not happen.

The best thing that could happen on this date would be _____

_____

_____

_____

The very worst thing that could happen on this date would be

_____

_____

_____

To make certain that this does not happen, I will _____

_____

_____

_____

6

Helping a Victim

When my sister was raped, the first thing I wanted
to do was crawl into my bed, pull the covers up
over my head, and cry. I didn't want to see any-
one. I didn't want to talk about it, and I certainly didn't want to
face my sister.

But, compelled by a sense of responsibility and a love for my
sister, I crawled out from under the covers and went to see her.
All the way to her house, I wondered what I would say. I hoped
and prayed that words of comfort and wisdom would fall from
my mouth. I was fairly composed by the time I got there.

Several cars were already in her driveway, so I knew that
friends and family had already begun to gather. I slowly walked
into her house, and when my sister turned to greet me, I burst
into tears. As we stood, holding each other tightly and crying
quietly, suddenly the horror of what she had just been through
seared through my heart and I knew I would never again be
quite the same.

It was almost like a funeral. People brought food and sat
around in small groups talking quietly. There was no laughter,
no chatter. We were bound by the tragedy of what had just
occurred. We all wanted to help, and we all desperately wanted
things to be normal again.

Trying to get things back to normal again is a common re-

> "There is nothing more isolating than the pain of violation. It forces victims to question themselves and their world because it destroys two essential beliefs: their sense of trust and their sense of control over their lives."—*The Crime Victims Book,* Dr. Morton Bard and Diane Sangrey

sponse from people trying to help rape victims, but it is not always the best one. While the most important thing you can offer a victim is love and support, you can learn other skills so that you will be most effective in helping a friend through this trauma.

While we are learning to avoid rape by being strong, self-confident, and assertive women, we also need to learn to help each other by being compassionate, sympathetic, and caring to the survivors.

Knowing how to help someone who has been raped should be part of every woman's basic skills. Just as we learn CPR, how to stop bleeding, or how to rescue a drowning person, we should learn the fundamentals of dealing with a rape victim. Support from friends and acquaintances can mean the difference between remaining traumatized for years or learning from the experience to reach a higher level of personal growth.

Dealing with someone who has been traumatized by a sexual assault is difficult. Our initial reaction usually is selfish. We feel sad that something like this has happened to someone we know, but we also feel vulnerable. Particularly if the rape victim is someone who lives or works close to us, our first thought is, It could have been me.

It *could* have been you. Or me. Because statistics show that one of every eight women in America has been raped, it becomes increasingly obvious that it can happen to any of us.

No one likes to face this fact or to be reminded of how fragile our lives are. By listening to my sister talk about her rape, I came face-to-face with the bitter reality that bad things do happen to good people and that there is no magical spirit that can keep us safe at all times.

In dealing with a victim, our own peaceful existence is threatened, at least temporarily. We want to turn away; we want everything calm and quiet again. But only by facing the reality of rape and dealing with its causes and consequences will we be able to put a stop to it.

But I Don't Want Anyone to Know

Only about half of the women who are raped ever tell anyone: friend, family, or authorities.

There are many reasons women do not report a rape or sexual assault. Because of the nature of the crime, victims often feel that somehow the rape was their fault.

Many are worried about how their families will react. According to a 1992 study by the National Victim Center, 69 percent of women who have been attacked feel that they would be blamed by others for having caused the rape. They may feel guilty about having left a bar or party with a man alone, about having dressed suggestively, or about having been drinking or taking drugs.

Helen knew that her parents did not approve of Richard, but with an impatient shake of her head she told herself she didn't care. They were so strict. They didn't want her to have any fun. She had told them that she was going to Sally's house, but instead Richard was going to pick her up at the mall. He had promised her a fun evening—"an evening she would never forget" is how he had put it—and Helen shivered with anticipation.

When Richard picked her up, he kissed her hard. "Ready?" he asked.

"Ready for what?" Helen laughed.

He looked at her sideways as he drove out of the parking lot. "Come on, Helen. I know you've been wanting it. Now's our big chance."

Suddenly Helen knew what he was talking about, and she began to shake. "No, Richard, I don't want it. Stop the car, I want to get out."

Richard only grabbed her arm and yanked her toward him. "Don't be a baby. If you didn't want it, why did you come tonight?"

He drove out in the country and stopped the car at the top of the hill on an old, seldom used dirt road. Helen had begun to cry, begging him to take her home, but he ignored her. It was only after he raped her that he took her home.

Helen stumbled out of the car, numb with shock and pain. When her mother opened the door, Helen fell inside and began to cry uncontrollably. Finally the story unfolded.

Her parents sat listening to her crying, and then her father said, "Well, Helen, we're sorry that this happened to you, but we told you not to go out with that boy. We knew that something like this would happen. I guess you've learned your lesson now."

Unfortunately, Helen's case is not unusual. Younger rape victims are often met with accusatory questions like, "Well, what did you expect, the way you were dressed?" These children who deserve our utmost care and concern are often made to feel that they are alone in the world with their guilt and their shame.

Younger women may decide not to tell anyone about a rape because they may feel that no one will believe them, particularly if the attacker was socially prominent or popular among her peers. Some women even choose not to report the crime because they do not want to get their attackers into trouble.

Some women do not report rapes because they feel helpless in a legal system that makes it difficult to convict rapists. Another deterrent to reporting these crimes is the lack of a law prohibiting the media from disclosing the names and addresses of rape victims. Without the guarantee of anonymity, these women are reluctant to take a chance on their names being reported in the news and people finding out about the crime. They want to forget this nightmare as quickly as possible and do not want to prolong the agony through the media.

Reporting a Rape

Reporting a rape is important, not only for the recovery of the victim but also for stopping the rapist. If a man rapes repeatedly and no one ever reports his crimes, he will gain more confidence and will suffer less fear of getting caught.

Rapes can be reported in various ways. According to Andera Parrot, author of *Acquaintance Rape and Sexual Assault Prevention*, a woman can give information to the police without having to give her name or press charges. She can press criminal charges, or she can also sue her attacker in civil court for pain, suffering, and recovery of therapy costs. If she is a student, the woman can and should report the crime to the school authorities.

Every time women do not report a rape, every time we do not support a victim, every time we help perpetuate the myth that men have a right to force sexual favors from a woman, every time we pretend to ourselves that rape is not a problem in our society, we are adding to the problem.

**Only 16 percent of rape victims report the crime to police.
—1992 study by National Crime Center**

How Can We Help?

The psychological effect of being the victim of a violent crime should never be underestimated. According to Shelley Neiderbach, Ph.D., founding president of Crime Victims' Counseling Services, Inc., rape victims will feel many different emotions, including guilt, rage, shame, humiliation, anxiety, fear, and hopelessness. It has been found that crime victims are ten times more likely than the average person to become severely depressed, even after ten years or more, and that the quality of their support system makes all the difference in the speed of their recovery.

Under any circumstances, rape is a severe trauma, and the victim should be treated as if she has lost a loved one. In many ways, rape is like a death.

Rape victims suffer disillusionment and are forced to face the reality of their mortality. For many of us it is the death of idealism, the loss of trust, the end of naiveté.

The *Ms.* magazine report on acquaintance rape says that 82 percent of women who had been raped said the experience had changed them forever.

Although a rape victim will almost always benefit from talking to a trained and experienced counselor, the role of a supportive friend should never be overlooked. There are many things you can say that will help, but the greatest gift you can give to a survivor is unconditional love and support.

Susan Salasin wrote in "Caring for Victims: An Interview with Steven Sharfstein," "There really is no substitute for compassionate outreach to victims. Concern must be indicated. . . . Be a good listener. The key, at least initially, is to be able to sit through some of the very painful feelings of a person in distress.

"Friends and family who support rape victims often tend to 'tune out' after the first couple of weeks. We all want things to return to normal as soon as possible and we often rationalize that 'she seems to be handling it pretty well.'"

The Crime Victims' Counseling Services in New York City found that 80 percent of those who helped crime victims suffered some of the same responses: "Feeling nervous or frightened; increased suspicion of people; feeling less safe at home or on the street. However, most supporters did not regret that the victim had turned to them."—Shelley Neiderbach, *Invisible Wounds*

To remain with the victim, continuing to talk about the attack and keeping it in the forefront of our thinking, prolongs our feelings of vulnerability. We usually wish the whole episode would somehow magically go away.

But to withdraw support too soon leaves the victim feeling isolated, unable to deal with the emotions that are still so raw for her. Realize that, for many women, recovery is a long journey. Stay with her as long as she needs you.

A victim needs help if she displays some of the following behaviors:

- inability to concentrate;
- a change in eating habits, either eating too much or too little;
- trouble sleeping.

If you have a friend who has been raped, help her by doing the following things:

- *Believe her and don't blame her.* Tell her that she has done the right thing because she is alive. Whatever she did, it was a smart choice.
- *Listen to her.* Let her pour out her story. Let her rage and storm, cry and scream.
- *Support her.* Be a witness for what she is feeling and saying without passing judgment. You can say, "I hear how enraged you are" rather than, "I don't blame you for being so angry. I would be too."
- *Call a rape crisis center immediately.* Chances of catching an assailant are much better if you can preserve evidence. Encourage your friend not to wash her hands, hair, or teeth, or even urinate. Save all the clothes that she was wearing at the time of the rape. A post-rape exam will try to get samples of blood, semen, saliva, and hair left by the rapist.
- *Go with her to the hospital, rape crisis center, police department, or wherever is necessary.* She may not realize she needs you, but she does.
- *Do physical things for her as you would do if someone were hurt*

or ill. Fix dinner, stay the night with her, clean the house, take care of the kids.

- *Be willing to confront your own past and deal with your own emotions.* Don't compound her trauma with your problem. Talk to other people about helping her. This is a traumatic experience for you, too.
- *Encourage the victim to get help from a trained trauma counselor.*
- *Help her to regain control of her life as quickly as possible.* This can start with little things. Let her decide what she wants to eat, what she will wear. Then move on to more important decisions, such as if and when to tell her family, whether she wants to prosecute or not.
- *Don't tell her to forget.* Let her work through this trauma the best way she knows how. There are no shortcuts to recovery. It takes time and courage to deal with the shock of a sexual attack.
- *Participate in a self-defense course with her.* This will give both of you a feeling of taking control, a feeling of power and strength. This is a safe and useful vehicle for venting your rage.

No one would ever wish agony on another. No one welcomes the pain of tragedy. But it is through trauma that many of us learn to grow spiritually and emotionally.

You can learn more about yourself from a few days of agony than you can from years of peaceful contentment. It is when we feel that we have hit rock bottom that we learn who we are and what we are made of. Hard times become an opportunity for growth.

When faced with tragedy, you can choose how you will let it affect you. You can let it beat you down and change you into an angry, bitter woman, or you can accept that it has happened—through no fault of your own—and learn. Tragedy can teach us compassion for victims who have gone before us and sympathy and understanding for those who will come after us.

Anyone who survives a rape—no matter how—deserves our respect. She has shown that a life force burns strongly within her.

The will to live is nothing anyone can teach or give to you. It is something you have to discover and nurture within yourself. Some people are born with a strong survival instinct and are able to fight for their lives with fierce determination; for others it is more difficult.

Rape Hotlines

Every state and most larger cities have rape crisis centers. To find these numbers, contact your local police department, YWCA, or health department.

7

For the Children

Margaret was a good soccer player. Even though she was only nine years old, she already had big plans about playing in high school. Every free minute that she had, she would be out in the backyard practicing dribbling and shooting goals.

On Thursday afternoon she told her mother that the coach had asked her to stay late so he could give her some extra help. "But you don't have to worry. He said he would bring me home too."

Margaret's mother smiled. "That's great, honey." She was fully supportive of her daughter's soccer goals, but as a single parent it was sometimes difficult to get her to all the extra practices.

It was after dark when Margaret finally got home. Her mother had begun to worry and was relieved to hear her come in the back door. "How was practice?" she called out, but Margaret merely mumbled "fine" and went into her room and closed the door.

Her mother went to the door. "Are you OK?" she asked.

Margaret answered quietly. "Yes. It was just a hard practice. I'm fine."

In the next few weeks it became apparent that Margaret was not fine. She seemed depressed and listless and, more disturbing, had suddenly lost interest in soccer. She didn't want to go to practice, didn't want to go to the games, and refused to talk about it.

Thinking that she was just going through a slump, her mother insisted that she continue to go. Finally it got so bad that her mother decided to talk to the coach herself. She got off work early and went to pick up Margaret at the soccer field.

It took her a few minutes to find Margaret. It appeared that the rest of the team had already left. Only Margaret and her coach were still there, and when she saw them Margaret's mother screamed. They were behind some trees—almost hidden from sight—and the coach had his hands all over the girl's body, pulling at her clothes. Margaret was crying silently.

In April 1992 new statistics on rape were published by the Crime Victims Research and Treatment Center. The numbers were staggering and depressing, for the figures on rape were a full five times greater than the 1985 Department of Justice statistics. Of all the facts reported in this study, however, none were more disturbing than the number of little girls who have been raped in this country.

Twenty-nine percent of the rapes occur when the victim is younger than eleven, and 32 percent occur between the ages of eleven and seventeen. That is, 61 percent of all rapes in America occur when the girls are seventeen years old and younger.

Talking with Children About Rape

I never imagined that I would have to sit down with my children and talk to them about rape. Sex, yes. I planned for years about how I would explain about the mystery of sex, but it wasn't until a few years ago that I realized that high numbers of children in this country were being raped.

As a responsible parent, I had no alternative but to speak to my children frankly about rape—what it means, who rapes, what they can do to protect themselves.

Rape is a difficult concept for children to grasp, particularly rape by someone they know, as happens in the vast majority of child rapes. The effect of rape on teens and children should not be underestimated. Many of these girls don't even know they have been raped. A girl may have consented to having sex with a teacher because she is unaccustomed to saying no to a voice of authority. It may be nearly impossible for her to assert herself enough to fight back simply because she feels confused, scared, or even guilty. Teens and children who have been raped sometimes run away from home or resort to drugs or alcohol. Some even commit suicide.

Talking to your kids about rape is as important as talking to them about drugs and alcohol, or sex and AIDs. Because there is so much misinformation and confusion about sex among adolescents, discussion about acquaintance rape is a necessity.

The basis for a discussion of rape or sex (or anything else of major consequence) has to be openness and honesty. You need to tell your children that:

- you will listen to them when they tell you things;
- you will believe them;
- you will be there for them.

Then you need to back up your words. Open communication between parents and children can save much heartache, yours and theirs. Take time to be with your children and truly talk with them. Don't just preach at them or lecture. Knowing they have a safe haven at home makes a big difference to kids.

Also, be aware of any changes in your child's behavior. If she (or he—boys can be rape victims also) is suddenly listless, begins to lose weight, or seems depressed, find out what's going on. Don't demand to know, just encourage her or him to talk; and check out her or his usual activities to find out if all is in order.

Talking with Younger Children (ages five to ten)

If you are a parent of a young child, you must talk to him or her about rape and sexual molestation. Boys *and* girls are vulnerable at this age. We cannot just sit back and hope and pray that this doesn't happen to our children; we must take preventive measures and teach our children how to protect themselves.

Remember that rape is a matter of power and that a rapist looks for someone weak and easily intimidated. Children fall into this category all too easily.

When you talk to your child, choose a time when you are relaxed and are not pressed to do anything or go anywhere, a time when your child is happy and rested. What you have to say is too important for it to land on sleepy ears.

You might tell your child some facts such as:

- Bad things happen to good people.
- There are people in the world that do bad things.
- There is good touching and bad touching. Only a doctor has the right to touch your private parts, and even then you can ask to have me there if it makes you feel better.
- Sometimes other big people touch children in their private places, and this makes the children feel bad. This is a bad thing.
- If someone ever makes you feel bad like that, you should tell them, "No! Leave me alone!" Even if it is someone you know and like. No one has the right to touch you in your private parts or to say things that make you uncomfortable.
- If someone ever makes you uncomfortable by touching you or talking to you about your private parts, tell me.

It is important that children become aware that there are people who can hurt them and do things to make them feel uncomfortable. *They need to know they have the right to tell people no! when they are made to feel uncomfortable.* You need to say this to them several times. It is a crucial concept for children to understand. Saying it just once will not be enough.

Children should understand that they should tell you any-thing that people say or do that makes them feel uncomfortable. They need to understand that you will listen to them and will take them seriously. You will have to prove yourself to your children on the last part; the only way you will get their trust is to earn it.

Children should also be told that if something like this hap-pens, *it is not their fault.* Child victims of sexual assaults almost always assume they have done something wrong.

If a child tells you about a situation that could indicate mo-lestation, don't overreact in front of him or her. If you go beserk, your child will be further traumatized. Act on it im-mediately but, if possible, make sure that your child is in a safe place away from you while you investigate.

Later, let your child know what you find out. ("Jane, re-member what you told me about your teacher? Well, he'd done the same thing to some other girls. He will not ever teach school again because what he does to children is very, very wrong. You will have a new teacher who is nice and will never make you feel uncomfortable.")

Talking with Older Children and Teenagers

Preteens and teens are particularly vulnerable because of their naiveté, their inexperience, and their innate belief that if they are good, bad things will not happen to them. These young people are also vulnerable because most are quick to trust people and to think they must have misunderstood intentions if things go wrong. They are also at risk because of the great number of new people coming into their lives—friends, teachers, coaches, or schoolmates. It's difficult to get to know them all well.

When you talk to your child, be as specific as possible. Don't resort to general statements like "Be careful" or "Just say no." You have to tell them what to be careful about and what to say no to.

You might begin by telling them what rape is. Your defini-tion will depend on the age of the child. Don't make the terms so technical and your approach so far over her or his head that the youngster won't know what you're talking about. Bring the discussion to your children's level. The trick, of course, is to make your children aware but not paranoid. The best way to do this is to be matter-of-fact. Even if you are boiling inside, don't show your children your anger about this situation. If you are scared to death, don't let your children see your excessive fear.

Listen to what your children say in response. You can tell a lot about their own fears by hearing what they tell you. In all discussions about rape, it is important to emphasize that this can happen with someone they know.

When your daughter begins to date, tell her:

- She has the right to the privacy of her own body. She does not have to let anyone touch her for any reason.
- She has the right to leave a date or a party at any time and come home if she wants.
- She is not responsible for her date's well-being. She does not have to have sex for any reason, including leading him on, his spending a lot of money on her, having had sex before, getting him so excited he can't control himself, or his threatening never to see her again or vowing to kill himself if she won't have sex.
- She does not have to pay for *anything* with sex. Her body and her privacy are hers and hers alone.

When your son begins to date, make sure he understands:

- Sex should be a wonderful outgrowth of a relationship based on love and respect.
- He should never force himself sexually on his date.
- If his date says no to sexual advances, assume that she means no and stop immediately
- If he forces himself on a girl or woman of any age against her wishes, he has committed rape and that rape is a criminal act.
- If he is convicted of rape, he will be sent to a juvenile home or to jail.

The encouraging—and ultimately frustrating—fact is that in many instances, *rape is a preventable crime*. We can do things to help girls learn to stay safe, but all of us—men and women, politicians, educators, religious and business leaders—must work together to stop this senseless violence against our children. Help is needed at all levels—individual, community, state, and national. You can do many things to help.

Helping As an Individual

- Educate yourself. Learn as much as you can about rape and self-defense. Take a self-defense class. Read books (see bibliography). Be a good role model, and talk to other women and girls. Help educate people about the problem and the solution.
- Get involved with the school in your community. Volunteer your time to help teach basic self-defense to girls in your school. This should involve all aspects of self-defense, from self-esteem to physical responses.
- Volunteer your time in helping to organize or run a girls' sports program. Many programs are already in place, so contact your local YWCA or school to find out where you can help or how to begin a program in your community.
- Talk to sons and daughters about sex and dating. Be open and honest, and let them know exactly what the issues are. Don't make them paranoid, but be sure they are aware of the problems and the solutions.
- Talk to groups about rape. You can talk to children in school groups, scout groups, or other community organizations, or to adult groups, telling them of the problem and what they can do to help.
- If you have children, take a long look at how you are raising them. Are you reinforcing the aggressive male-passive female relationships? Do you encourage your daughter to stand up for herself, even if it means that things are not as smooth and quiet in the family? Do you encourage your daughter to become involved in sports and exercise? Do you encourage your son to develop all sides of his personality, the artistic and nurturing as well as the physical and aggressive?

Helping As a Community

- Learn the statistics about rape in your community. Determine the demographics of the crimes. Who is being raped and where? These statistics are generally available through the local police department. Target these areas. If rape occurs in the local park, have better lighting installed. If it happens on the streets, hire extra law enforcement officials or private security personnel.

- Find funds for better safety. Security is often expensive, but no price is too high for the safety of our children. If community funds are not available, go to the private sector. When you talk to business people about donating money for these changes, do your homework first. Know your statistics. Target one or two specific changes that you want to bring about and know what they will cost. Do not be hysterical or overly emotional; stay calm and rational. If you get turned down, stay polite and don't become discouraged. There is a lot of money in this country, and this is an important issue. Simply keep trying. Grants or government funds may also be available.

- Education in the schools is a crucial step in preventing the rape of school-age children. Sponsor teachers or lecturers to come into the schools and talk to both boys and girls, to a parent-teacher organization, and to educators.

- Talk to the school board about including safety and self-defense curriculum in the schools. This curriculum should be mandatory for all students, and it can be included in health or physical education classes. Discussions about protecting the privacy of your own body and how to communicate assertively should be included during elementary school years.

- Get the community involved in helping girls realize their own strength and potential. Ask local health clubs or karate studios to offer special classes for girls. Let it be fun for these girls. Learning to be strong and independent is an exhilarating experience.

Helping As a State

- Talk to legislators about passing state laws requiring colleges and universities to establish clear, concise codes prohibiting rape on campus and listing penalties if violated.
- Pass laws making education about acquaintance rape mandatory for *all* college freshmen—men and women.
- Work with fraternities and sororities in your state colleges. Encourage them to have educational speakers and seminars about date rape.
- Require colleges to publish and make available campus crime statistics.

Helping As a Nation

- Pass laws prohibiting the media from publishing the names and addresses of rape victims.
- Support groups such as these with time and money:

National Institute on Rape
Post Office Box 2325
Berkeley, CA 94708

U.S. Department of Health and Human Services
National Center for the Prevention and Control of Rape
National Institute of Mental Health
5600 Fishers Lane
Rockville, MD 20857

Part Two

Survival Skills

Rape is a preventable crime, and we can take specific actions to protect ourselves. The second section of this book is designed to teach you these skills, but you must realize that many of them will not come automatically to you. Speaking assertively is a skill you may need to work on. Learning to kick with force and power is something you will have to practice, and exercising and getting into shape is something you will have to do the rest of your life.

To have a life without fear, it is important that you learn these basic survival skills. For the most part, they will greatly enhance your life in many areas.

Learning to communicate effectively can only enrich your relationships. Getting in shape will make you feel more alert and alive and will raise your energy level. Developing your intuitive powers will help you learn more about yourself, your creativity, and the potential that lies within you.

Basic to the successful use of all survival skills is a will to live. This cannot be taught or given. It is within us all, and we must nurture it.

Being liberated from fear gives us the opportunity to embrace life fully and completely.

8

Using Your Sixth Sense: Intuition, Visualization, and Awareness

Severaly ears ago I was on my way to visit my doctor at a downtown office building. The appointment was for two o'clock, and I had plenty of time as I parked my car and went into the building. As I stood waiting for the elevator, a man walked up beside me. He was nice looking, wore a suit, and carried a briefcase; there was no apparent reason for alarm. Suddenly I had an overwhelming sense of dread and an almost physical sensation of danger. My breathing quickened, and I felt panic start in the pit of my stomach.

When the elevator door opened, he motioned for me to go inside. But something was telling me that it would be disastrous for me to get into the elevator. Feeling stupid, I mumbled something about being in the wrong building. He looked a little puzzled but shrugged and entered the elevator. My relief was almost palpable when he was gone.

I never saw him again, never saw his picture on a wanted poster at the post office, and never saw his face in the newspapers; but I am convinced that if I had gotten on the elevator with that man, I would have been in great danger.

All of us have extra senses that tell us things our common five senses cannot. We can learn to develop these senses so they essentially become our internal alarm system.

There are three main elements of this internal system. First is the use of intuition to let us know when we are in danger. All of us have had intuitive feelings at one time or another. It can be a simple feeling that you are going to have a really good day, or as precise as knowing that a friend you haven't heard from in a long time is going to call today.

The second element is visualization. Creative visualization is a powerful psychological tool used by different kinds of people, from professional athletes and performers to astronauts and doctors.

The third element is increasing your awareness of events and people around you.

These three things will help keep you safe. They are *preventive* measures. If you work at developing them, they can help prevent the tragedy of rape or sexual assault.

How? By listening to your intuitive voice, you will be able to "read" people better. You will have a better feeling about people and situations you should avoid and will act more quickly when you feel you are in danger.

By learning to visualize, you will pinpoint your greatest fears and will learn that you are not helpless. If you are able to visualize yourself acting in an assertive, controlled manner, then you will know how to respond if you are ever attacked. The power of creative visualization is that we can become anything that we can visualize.

Heightened awareness will make you more in tune with your surroundings. You will no longer walk around in a daze, and the image you will project is one of being alert and in control.

Intuition

As I researched for this book, I continually looked for some common element present in all sexual attacks on women, something that each of the women had experienced. I suppose I was hoping I'd find a key that would let me say, If you do this or you don't do that, it will prevent you from being attacked.

Of course, it is not that simple. All kinds of women are sexually assaulted. All kinds of men assault women under all kinds of circumstances. But there does seem to be a common element in all cases.

Almost all of the women I talked to and case studies I read indicated that these women experienced a "funny feeling," an internal warning system that suggested that all was not well.

This funny feeling goes by a variety of names: a sixth sense, a hunch, intuition, a gut feeling, a personal radar. For women, using and listening to this voice may mean the difference between walking blindly into a dangerous situation and stopping ourselves before danger approaches. You might call this your "inner angel."

Your inner angel is a feeling within you that warns of danger. Learn to listen to it. Your life may depend on it.

Many police and military personnel will tell you that this sixth sense has saved their lives on more than one occasion. Once you learn to use it, you learn to depend on it.

Laurie Nadel in her book *Sixth Sense* reported that a former New York City police officer found that hunches are an essential part of staying alive on the streets.

Over and over again women who were assaulted said they experienced a feeling that something was wrong. This was particularly true of women assaulted by an acquaintance. These women ignored their own inner feelings and accepted dates with men who made them uncomfortable. Sometimes they continued to ignore this inner voice as the date progressed, and their discomfort grew until the date finally erupted in an attempted, or completed, rape.

Why? Why would a woman continue to ignore her feelings and keep up the pretense that nothing was going wrong? Much of this response comes from how we were raised and our desire to form relationships. We have been taught to be nice, to be charming, to please a man; and it takes a great deal of courage and self-assertion to interrupt a "romantic" evening by going home for no other reason than you had a "funny feeling."

Go back and look at the list of characteristics of a date rapist (see page 73). If you start to have a funny feeling about going out with someone, check his personality traits with this list.

Men who are angered by small acts of assertion such as opening your own door or ordering for yourself are sending loud, strong signals to you. Pick up on these signals, and listen to your inner voice. If it is telling you to leave, do so as quickly as you can. Trust your inner voice. If it tells you to leave, don't stay and try to figure out why; leave first, and think about it later.

One element about intuition is that it comes with a sense of urgency. You may have had a nagging feeling all evening, but as more imminent danger approaches, this feeling will come with a clear signal that you need to act *now!*

We cannot afford to ignore our inner angel. If this one thread is common to all victims and survivors, then we need to pay attention to it.

It is true that some people are more naturally intuitive than others. It is also true that anyone can develop his or her intuition powers and learn to use them. Becoming more intuitive will enhance your life. In addition to keeping you safe, a greater sense of intuition will help in all areas of your life.

Highly intuitive people are said to be creative, self-confident, curious, and independent. Many of these characteristics will help prevent sexual assault.

It is the strong, self-confident, independent woman—alert, aware, and in tune with her senses—whom we need to mimic.

It is this part of ourselves that we need to listen to in a dangerous situation.

You can learn to develop and hone your intuitive skills. Like learning any other kinds of skill, though, don't expect it to come to you without a little work or practice.

Learning to Be Intuitive

Intuition is a subject that makes many people nervous because it goes beyond the realm of the ordinary. Webster defines intuition as "the immediate knowing of something without the conscious use of reasoning." We are so accustomed to using our powers of reasoning that we sometimes ignore or squelch the intuitive part of our brains.

> If you experience a strong feeling when you first meet someone, pay attention to it.

To be able to hear your inner angel more clearly in times of trouble, it is helpful to listen to your intuition at other times as well.

Before you can use your inner angel, you've got to be able to recognize her. All of us have gut feelings about people. Often, when we first meet some-one we will either like him instantly or take an immediate dislike to him. Love at first sight is a good example of this feeling.

If you experience a strong feeling when you first meet some-one, pay attention to it; this is your inner angel talking to you. Stop for a moment and think about how you feel. Can you identify the place in your body where the feeling is strongest? Is it in your "gut," your mind, your heart, your feet? People experience intuition in different places.

How did you look and sound when you were experiencing these feelings? Were you having any physical sensations such as increased heart rate, a prickly feeling, or a sudden chill?

If you are able to recognize certain signals when you are getting clear intuitive messages, it will be easier for you to identify them again later.

If you find yourself in a situation where your inner angel begins to nag at you, take stock of the situation. Ask yourself some questions:

- What is bothering me? Try to be as specific as possible.
- How am I reacting physically? Am I cold or hot all of a sudden? Does my skin feel funny?
- What am I afraid of?
- Do I feel I need to act immediately?
- How would my ideal strong, assertive woman handle this situation?

It is possible to increase your intuitive powers by practicing in a safe, soothing environment. Listening to quiet music, meditating, doing rhythmic exercise such as walking, running, swimming, yoga, tai chi, or simply sitting still while listening to your own thoughts are all activities that are good for increasing intuitive thought.

Because your inner angel can be so important in keeping you safe, you owe it to yourself to develop your intuitive skills as strongly as possible. Trust is a major part of using your intuition. If you don't trust yourself, it will be difficult to trust your intuition.

Visualization

In my mind's eye, the man is of medium build, pale, and sinister looking. He grabs me roughly by the elbow as I hurry from the library toward my car.

"What's your hurry?" he growls in my ear.

I gasp, and a scream wells in my throat. My heart is pounding so hard I think it will burst out of my chest. Panic grips at me.

I breathe deeply as I spin around to face him and yell—a full-throated noise coming from deep within me.

"Get your hands off me!" I start to pull away.

His grip tightens on my arm as he silently begins to pull me toward the alley.

I relax momentarily in his grip, actually taking a step toward him. He turns around, surprise on his face, and for a second he lessens his grip on my arm.

At that instant I yell again, "Get out of my face! You picked the wrong woman, you son of a bitch!" I pull back my free arm, tighten my fingers, and jab them straight into his eyes. My fingers penetrate. I am in total control of the situation.

He screams in surprise and agony and immediately releases me as his hands fly to his face.

Free of his grasp, I grab his shoulder, pivot, and bring my elbow full force across his jaw. His head is thrown backward. Still holding on to his shoulder, I raise my knee up high and stomp down on his knee with as much force as I can. He falls to the ground, clutching his knee.

I am yelling, this time "Help! Help!" and stand watching him for a moment, my breath coming in great gasps, still tense and ready to strike again if necessary. But he has had enough. Whimpering and sobbing with terror on his face, he drags himself away from me as quickly as possible.

He doesn't have far to go. My screams have brought people running, including a police officer who immediately puts handcuffs on my would-be assailant and drags him away.

This episode happened only in my mind, but I have played it over and over again, varying the time, the place, the attack, and the defense. Sometimes I am in bed and wake with someone hovering over me; sometimes I am on an empty elevator. Each time I finish out the scenario. I imagine in great detail how I would feel, how I would take control of the situation, what kind of tactics I would use, the physical maneuvers that would be necessary, what I would say. Always, always, I end up in control of the situation, and my attacker looks terrified and is caught so that he will never terrorize women again.

All of us wonder how we would actually react if attacked. If we have been attacked before, we wonder what we could do differently next time.

The best way to assure ourselves of a powerful, appropriate response is to visualize different attacks and then imagine exactly how we would best deal with the situation.

The art and science of visualization is a powerful tool used by many different kinds of people. Shakti Gawain says in her book *Creative Visualization* that there are three important elements in successful visualization: desire, belief, and acceptance.

In essence, visualization is the practice of making something come true by imagining it in your mind in great detail. This is a method often used by athletes who imagine themselves running faster, hitting harder, jumping higher, or whatever they need to do to accomplish their goal.

These same methods can be used by all of us to enhance the probability of a successful response to an attack.

If we can imagine in our minds exactly what we would do in a terrifying and stressful situation, if it actually happens to us, our brains will be less likely to freeze and go blank. If our minds have handled it before, the situation will at least be vaguely familiar and our response will be more effective.

To use visualization most effectively, we need to imagine the situation with as much detail as possible and to believe in our response. I truly believe I could stop an attacker using a series of techniques such as eye strike, elbow strike, and a kick to the knee while yelling and causing a scene and drawing people toward me. I know I will be scared. My heart starts to pound just thinking about it, but I also know that I am capable of taking care of myself. I believe in myself and will react with power and strength if attacked.

We don't need to be paranoid about our safety, nor do we need to be preoccupied and continuously think about being attacked. Through education, creative visualization, and keeping ourselves strong and fit, we can become more aware, act assertively, and greatly increase the level of our safety. This will release us from a cloying fear and paranoia and will allow us to live our lives fully and safely.

Essential to successful self-defense is a bit of advance strategic planning. If you can imagine a variety of strategies in advance, chances are much greater that you will carry through with them successfully.

- Have a clear goal in mind—that you escape unharmed.
- Be able to make a quick assessment of the degree of danger

in the situation. Is it a verbal attack? A strong physical one? Does he have a weapon?

- Have the skills necessary to carry out a number of different strategies—yelling and speaking assertively, running away, retaliating with appropriate self-defense maneuvers.
- Be mentally and emotionally prepared to carry through with these strategies.

Increasing Your Awareness

At the end of a long day at work, it is easy to put our minds on automatic and go through the motions of our daily lives. We may ride the train home in a blur, go to the grocery store, or walk back to our apartment. Unaware and oblivious to our surroundings, we act as if we are in a fog.

When we are sluggish, lethargic, and unaware of what is going on around us, we are also most vulnerable. Being aware of your surroundings can increase the level of your safety significantly.

Unless you are in a place where you consider yourself safe, you cannot indulge in the luxury of being unaware. Know what is going on around you. Watch people. Try to guess who they are and what they do. It will keep you alert, and the more you watch people, the better you will be able to read them.

> Being aware of your surroundings can increase the level of your safety significantly.

Many games and exercises will increase your powers of awareness and observation. When you first walk into a room, take immediate stock of the situation. Look around you. Notice the number of people in the room. Visually search for any suspicious-looking characters. Check out the doors. Where would you exit if you had to escape? What is the level of danger in this room?

Think what fun this could be when you're dressed in your exquisite evening gown and have just entered a room full of beautiful people. Imagine their surprise if they could hear what you were thinking. If you can do it in a relatively safe environment, it will serve you in good stead when you are in a most dangerous spot.

As you walk down the street, size up the men you meet. If you had to defend yourself against one of them, how would you do it? Would you go for the eyes? The knees? The groin? Is he so big and out of shape that immediately running away would be your best defense?

Look around you. Is help close by? If you scream, is there anyone close enough to hear you? Are there stores open along the street where you could safely hide until someone picked you up? Is there a phone where you could call for help?

It's all a mental exercise, all with a distinct purpose.

IN A NUTSHELL

1. In a successful self-defense, you need to use all of your senses, not just the common five.
2. Almost all women who have been raped have reported having an intuitive feeling that something was wrong before the rape occurred.
3. Highly intuitive people are said to be creative, self-confident, curious, and independent, many of the same characteristics that will help prevent sexual assault.
4. Trust your intuition; it may save your life.
5. The best way to assure a powerful, appropriate response is to visualize different attacks and then imagine exactly how best to deal with the situation.
6. Being thoroughly aware of your surroundings can significantly increase the level of your safety.
7. Unless you are in a place where you consider yourself safe, you cannot indulge in the luxury of being lethargic and unaware.

Note: Some people are more in tune with their sixth sense than others, but all of us can work to develop our extra senses. We can do this by sharpening our observation skills, by working on our intuition, or by learning to visualize many different actions and situations.

Exercise 1

After you meet someone for the first time, take a few minutes to write down your thoughts about him. List all the concrete things you know about this person: where he works, his hobbies, what he looks like, what he is studying, where he lives. Now list your intuitive feelings about him. Do you feel safe with him? Does he seem sensitive to your feelings? Does he seem overpowering? Would you suspect he has a dangerous temper? These are probably things you don't *know* about him, but you probably have some gut feelings about it. Listen to your inner angel.

Exercise 2

Finding a safe spot.

For any of us to grow to our own potential, it is essential that we do it from a place of safety. Anyone who is fearful cannot devote the necessary time, energy, and effort to grow inwardly. As individuals and as women, safety is not a luxury but an essential part of our basic human rights.

To find a place of safety is, sadly, not always an easy thing to do. For many women, even their homes are places of fear.

Within ourselves, however, we all have a spot of inner sanctity. This is a place within our hearts and souls from which we can begin to grow.

To find your safe spot, find a place where you feel physically safe. Depending on your circumstances, this might be your home or perhaps a public—but safe—place such as a library or museum. Sit quietly for a few moments and let your thoughts wander. Do not try to stop thinking, for that is impossible, but direct thoughts and emotions inward until you feel safe and secure inside. Imagine what this place would look like if you could see it, and imprint this image in your memory.

This is your inner sanctuary. No one can take this away from you. No one knows what it looks like or feels like except you. When you are troubled or in danger, go back to this spot within yourself, for it is here that your inner angel lives. Listen to her. Learn from her.

Exercise 3

All of us probably have certain secret fears, situations that occur to us over and over again. Take this secret fear and bring it out into the open. Write down the entire scenario—where you are and exactly what happens minute by minute. Envision yourself taking control of the situation and describe your every maneuver and how you felt after every move. Work with this visualization until you are perfectly satisfied with it, that you responded as a strong, assertive, self-sufficient woman.

Exercise 4

Draw an escape route on paper. Sit down and actually draw out the route you would take to safety if you were attacked in your home, your place of work, your dorm room, the library, or any other place you frequent. If an attacker came in your bedroom door, is there another door to the room through which you could escape? Can you jump out the window? When you get out of the bedroom, would you run to the front door? The back door? Can you get out the door quickly, or would you be trapped while fumbling with the lock? Do you have a mobile phone you could grab on the way out to call for help? Try to think of as many alternatives as possible.

Exercise 5

On a piece of paper, immediately write down what your roommate (child, husband, mother, or anyone else that you live with) had on the last time you saw her. Describe her in as much detail as possible, as if you were giving this information to the police.

Tell how tall she is, how much she weighs, color and length of hair, the kind of clothes she had on (in detail), and facial characteristics.

Police will tell you that the most useful clues in identifying someone are characteristics that make that person stand out from all the rest. Birthmarks, scars, tattoos, unusual facial features are all good characteristics to report. Also try to include information about how the person walks, how she carries herself, or any quirks that make her different. Does your child sort of skip when she walks? Does your mother have one shoulder that droops. Does your roommate walk with a slight limp?

You might be surprised at how little you remember about someone you live with. Even mothers who help their kids dress in the morning sometimes do it so automatically by midday they can't even remember what they have on.

Sharpen your awareness skills by starting with the obvious. Be able to describe those closest to you.

Describe in detail your roommate (or child or spouse), including what she had on the last time you saw her. _____

_____

_____

_____

_____

9

Communication

Cindy met Stephen in a freshman English class. During the first few weeks of school, she chatted with him after class and was pleased when he finally asked her to go to the football game on Saturday.

They had a great time together at the game, and when he suggested that they go back to his dorm room before they went out for dinner, she readily agreed. She had drunk more than she was used to and the thought of getting out of the sun for a while and sitting somewhere cool sounded good.

When they got to his room, Stephen closed the door and locked it behind him. A warning bell went off in Cindy's head. Immediately Stepehen started kissing her and pressing his body against hers.

Cindy began to feel uncomfortable. She was enjoying kissing Stephen and she liked him, but she felt a little scared that things were going so fast. She wanted to say something, but she didn't want to ruin the whole day.

She tried to wiggle away from him a little, but he seemed to only get more excited as she moved. Finally Cindy pushed him away.

"Ummm, I don't think I'm ready for this," she mumbled.

Stephen seemed to be in a frenzy and pulled her toward him again. "Sure you are. Come on, don't get cold on me now."

Cindy allowed herself to be kissed some more, her eyes squeezed shut and her heart pounding. She didn't want to appear cold, but she was beginning to feel that things were getting out of control and she was a little scared. As she felt Stephen's hand reaching for her crotch, she again pushed away. This time there was no uncertainty in her voice.

She looked Stephen right in the eye. "Stephen, I don't want to have sex with you now. I like you and I like kissing you, but I don't want to go any farther than that. Besides, I feel a little uncomfortable in a locked room with you all by myself. Let's slow down, OK?" and she continued to look at him in the eye.

With an obvious effort, Stephen quieted his breathing and calmed himself. He sat down heavily on the bed, looking dejected. "OK, OK. But next time say something before I get myself so worked up. Once I get started, it's hard to stop."

Communication As a Survival Skill

Clear communication is one of the most important skills you can learn for keeping yourself safe from sexual assault. There is so much miscommunication about sex that sometimes we are a bit confused as to how we feel and what is best to say. Sometimes we are also bewildered by our own reactions to circumstances, particularly in the case of an attack from a date or an acquaintance.

It is difficult for many women to communicate directly. We are concerned about hurting people's feelings or about alienating someone we know. But clear communication is a skill that will serve you well in many circumstances, from staying safe from sexual assault to developing open, honest relationships.

By learning to listen to ourselves, to communicate openly and directly with a date, and to use assertive, forceful communication with an attacker, we can thwart some sexual attacks verbally.

The Danger of Not Communicating

It is hard to speak our minds clearly or forcefully, but it seems particularly difficult for a woman to communicate directly, especially when relationships are involved.

Too often we don't say anything because we are afraid. We fear a confrontation; we fear rejection; we fear hurting someone's feelings.

"Fear is the greatest block to power and honesty. When it comes to relationships, we are usually most afraid of criticism, conflict, and failure."—Maria Arapakis, author of *SoftPower*

Keeping our mouths shut is an avoidance behavior. Although not saying anything may seem like the safest way to avoid a confrontation, in the long run it may cause problems and lack of control over a situation.

If Cindy had not stopped Stephen when she had, it would have become increasingly difficult to get him to stop later. But by clearly stating what she wanted and did not want, Cindy was able to control what was becoming a dangerous situation for her.

Speaking your mind is an issue of self-confidence and responsibility. It takes courage to speak up and set limits, for in verbalizing what you want, you are opening yourself up to criticism and alienation. As long as you silently hope that a partner, friend, or date wants the same things you want, you can postpone a confrontation.

It was only when Stephen became more and more insistent and Cindy began to fear for her safety that she found the courage to speak her mind.

> "Silence implies consent. People are not mind readers. While bringing a concern out into the open never guarantees a resolution, saying nothing almost always guarantees more of the same."—Maria Arapakis, *SoftPower*

Communicating with Yourself

To be effective in telling someone how you feel about something, it is important for you to *know* how you feel. Examining your thoughts and feelings is a crucial first step to communicating effectively with others.

Knowing what you want can sometimes be as confusing for you as it is for your date. If a woman waits until the heat of the moment to decide what she wants, she will not be thinking clearly. Maria Arapakis says that "when emotions run high, your thinking becomes jammed, your perceptions distorted, your intuition blocked and your behavior disabled. Flooded with fear, you retreat. And when you retreat, you lose control."

A loss of control in a dangerous situation can mean the difference between staying safe and getting raped. When things happen suddenly, you will be feeling many conflicting emotions at once. Cindy liked Stephen and liked kissing him. She didn't want anything to disrupt the good time they were having, but she didn't want to have intercourse with him either. At first she was confused as to what to say. It was only when she was pushed and she began to feel fearful that she could clear her head well enough to know she did not want to have sex with Stephen and to speak forcefully enough to make him understand.

To prevent confusion in the heat of the moment, take some time to think about what you are looking for in a relationship, what you are *not* looking for, and what sort of limits you want to set for yourself and for your date.

The limits you set will depend on your own values, expectations, and lifestyle. Certain factors, however, must be considered when you set your limits, not the least of which is the threat of AIDS or pregnancy. Your limits may vary depending on whom you are with, where you are, and whether or not you have had anything to drink. If you take some time beforehand to set guidelines for yourself and your dating habits, you will be much more likely to follow them, even under stressful situations.

For instance, you may tell yourself that if you are going to have anything to drink, you will not have *any* sexual contact with anyone—no kissing, no slow dancing, nothing. Or you may tell yourself that if you have anything to drink, you will always stay with a group of people.

If you've been out with a guy several times and you really like him and enjoy sexual contact, you might tell yourself that petting is OK, but the clothes must stay on.

Only you know what you want. Only you know when you begin to get uncomfortable. Take some time before you go out, though, to decide what you really do want.

"When you say 'yes,' be sure you first know what you're agreeing to. You can be friendly but forceful. If he continues to ignore your wishes, don't worry about being polite. If you need to yell or hurt him to attract help or get away, do it. Forget about being a 'nice girl.'"—Robin Warshaw, *I Never Called it Rape*

Listen to Your Body

If you listen to your body, you will find it to be an excellent barometer of your emotions. Our bodies have an uncanny way of warning us when danger is near. All of us have experienced that prickly skin feeling when things are not as they should be.

Our bodies often react to danger faster than our minds, particularly if we are under the influence of drugs or alcohol.

Common physical symptoms indicating danger include:

- tightness of muscles;
- change in breathing (either quickened or slowed);
- change in body temperature (either flushed or cold).

Use these feelings as an inner alarm system. Your body is talking to you. Listen carefully.

If you feel uncomfortable in a situation, buy yourself enough time to figure out what is bothering you. If you are with a date who begins to get physical, start talking about something long enough for you to figure out how you feel about this. If you are not interested in having a sexual relationship with this man, now is the time to say so, not twenty minutes from now when things have really heated up.

He Thinks/She Thinks

Because so much communication is nonverbal, what you wear and how you act can sometimes be interpreted differently from how you intended it. Nonverbal communication between men and women is often particularly tricky because we read things so differently.

If a girl has a good figure and loves clothes, she might think it's fun to dress in a tight blouse and short skirt. She may think she is not sending out any message except, "Hey! Look at me, I'm cute."

Her date may read it altogether differently. Seeing her dressed provocatively, he may think that she's trying to arouse him and is offering to have sex with him.

If a woman touches a man first—holds his hand, strokes his cheek, or makes some other physical connection—he might read this as a sign she wants sex. She may only be doing this as a sign of affection.

Tremendous problems arise when men and women do not communicate well with each other. This is particularly true of sex because we are so hesitant to talk openly about the subject. Because we often rely on subtle hints and body language, clear understanding is even more difficult.

She thinks: I can't believe I fit into a size 6!
He thinks: She poured herself into that dress. She must be pretty hot for me.

She thinks: It's the man's place to pay for a date.
He thinks: I'm not paying for all this stuff without getting something back.

She thinks: I'm a liberated woman. I'll ask him out.
He thinks: She must be pretty horny if she has to do the asking.

She thinks: It would be cheaper for him if we went back to his place rather than go out. He would probably appreciate that.
He thinks: Great! She must really want it bad if she agreed to come to my place.

She thinks: One more drink won't hurt. I don't want him to think I'm some high school kid.
He thinks: One more drink and she won't put up much of a fight. She'll never remember what happened.

Communicating with a Date or an Acquaintance

It is particularly difficult for a woman to defend herself from rape when she knows the assailant. We like to believe that we will be safe with men we know. The vast majority of case studies from women who have been raped by an acquaintance start off with the woman saying, "I couldn't believe it was happening."

Admittedly, talking to your date about sex is a tricky subject. Even *talking* about sex implies that you think that is what he has on his mind, or it is what's on your mind. When you bring up the subject, he may laugh at you, get angry, act self-righteous, and accuse you of being presumptuous. But try to keep the big picture in mind. Many of his reactions might be a result of embarrassment.

It's better to look a little foolish than to be sorry you didn't.

It is unfortunate that a frank discussion of sex has to be a part of the initial stages of a relationship, but it is a fact of life. To be open and honest about how you feel about sexual relations is a necessity of the times we live in. Setting honest limits with yourself and with the men you have relationships with is a key to staying safe and healthy. If you are raped, you risk not only great psychological damage, but also the possibility of acquiring AIDs or becoming pregnant.

> Setting honest limits with yourself and with the men you have relationships with is a key to staying safe and healthy.

If you are able to communicate clearly and effectively, there will be no confusion or misunderstanding about how you feel. When you are able to set limits, chances are much greater that you will get what you want.

Suppose you've been going out with a boy for a couple of months, and he asks you to go to the mountains with him for the weekend with a group of friends. You really like him, and you would really love to go to the mountains. You could:

a. Go and pray that nothing bad happens to you;

b. Agree to go but tell him that you are not ready to have sex with him and that you would like to drive your own car;

c. Laugh at him and tell all your friends he only has one thing on his mind;

d. Tell him that you would love to go but that you don't feel comfortable doing it because you don't know him that well, so maybe another time.

Choice *a* is not a wise decision. You are placing yourself in a vulnerable position with no way out. Choice *c* is also not a good one. You don't have to be so paranoid that you think every boy who asks you out is going to rape you. Choices *b* and *d* are both possibilities, with choice *d* clearly the safest.

But if you decide to go or if you decide not to go, be open and honest about your decision. If you really care about this person, tell him why you have chosen not to go. If he's worth getting to know well, he'll understand. If he has a temper tantrum, he's probably not anyone you want to be with anyway.

If you decide to go, set up guidelines with him before you go. Make sure you both have similar expectations for the weekend. And read him carefully. Does he really agree with your stipulations? Can you trust him? Do you know the other friends?

Staying safe does not necessarily mean hiding in your closet. It does mean communicating clearly and effectively so that your expectations and those of your date are not misunderstood.

Calling It Rape

If you are with someone who ignores what you want and by force or the threat of force coerces you into having sex against your will, then let him know in no uncertain terms that you consider this rape and that you will prosecute.

Neither of you may consider him a criminal, but *as soon as a woman says no and a man continues to force himself on her, he becomes a criminal*. If he continues to fondle you, touching your breasts or genitals against your will, it is considered sexual assault. If penetration occurs with penis, fingers, or any object, then it is rape.

Nowhere is clear communication more essential than at this juncture. Many men are under the mistaken assumption that women liked to be forced sexually or that when they say no, they really means yes.

Make it perfectly clear that you are very serious. When you say no, you mean just that, and if he continues to force himself on you, you will consider his actions criminal.

He must understand that you are serious, and you must understand that if you are going to be able to defend yourself successfully, you must communicate clearly and assertively.

Communicating Assertively

Whether you are talking to a stranger on the street, an acquaintance who is getting forceful, or an ex-husband who has a twisted notion about reclaiming former sexual rights, speak firmly and directly.

If you use a neutral tone, it will help you calm down. It will also make it difficult for him to predict what you are going to do. If you can remain in control of your voice, you will at least sound as if you are in control of the situation. Struggle not to sound overly angry or fearful, both of which indicate a loss of control. And try very hard not to cry. Remember, you are in control. There will be time for tears later.

Communication experts point out that a low pitch is an indicator of power, while a high pitch is usually associated with flighty females and children.

You will also sound more powerful if you speak in commands and statements. Begging and pleading will only fuel an attacker's feeling of power, something you want to avoid at all costs.

Not only must your voice sound powerful, but your body language must support the impression. Ten percent of communication comes from our voice, 30 percent from other sounds we make, and 60 percent from our body language. It is important to present a complete image of control and power, supported by a firm, low-pitched voice and a strong, confident body. Even if you are quaking in your boots and you are only pretending to be in control, never let an attacker know that you are fearful.

Eye contact indicates you are not afraid. When attacked on the street or threatened by an acquaintance, look directly at him. It shows that you have courage.

Always speak slowly and calmly. A sudden hysterical outburst can spark an unwanted reaction from a nervous assailant, particularly if he is carrying a weapon. If you quietly reassure him that you will do whatever he says, he may soon feel that he does not need the weapon and may put it down.

If you are attacked on the street and there are people close by, try to make eye contact with one of them and speak directly to him or her. Don't just yell "Help!" or "Fire!" Give this person specific directions as to what to do. For example, say, "I'm being attacked. Find a phone, and call 911. Hurry!" People are much more likely to respond to a direct command than they are to a general cry for help.

Your Voice As a Weapon

Your voice can be a powerful weapon. A potential attacker does not want attention drawn to himself or his victim, so if you yell forcefully before an attack begins, you have a good chance of scaring him off.

There is a difference between a yell and a scream. A scream is an involuntary screech of anger or fear, and a yell is a loud outcry. Screams imply hysteria whereas a yell serves as a warning sign to the attacker that you know exactly what you are doing. Martial artists include a loud *kiya!* with every important strike or kick. This serves many purposes, all of which are equally beneficial to the woman practicing or using self-defense techniques. A *kiya!* is a loud gutteral yell that comes from deep within the body. If nothing else, this will startle or scare an opponent and give him the impression that you know what you are doing.

Yelling in this manner also helps expel breath. Often when people are frightened, they tend to hold their breath. This makes it much more difficult to fight back effectively.

So a loud yell of any sort will serve the purpose of startling your attacker and will force you to breathe, thus making your physical response more effective.

IN A NUTSHELL

1. Clear, strong communication is one of the strongest deterrents to rape.
2. Women have a difficult time communicating directly because we don't want to hurt someone's feelings or we fear criticism, confrontation, or rejection.

3. Silence implies consent. It is important to say what we mean, because people are not mind readers.
4. It's important to communicate with a date about our sexual expectations before we go out.
5. If a man continues to force himself on us in spite of our clear communication that we want him to stop, we must tell him we consider it rape.
6. Assertive communication is done in a steady, neutral voice supported by strong body language.
7. Do not plead or beg with a rapist. Talk in statements and commands.
8. Forty percent of our communication comes from voice and other sounds we make, 60 percent from body language.
9. Making eye contact with people indicates courage and self-assurance.

Note: Learning to communicate effectively takes a lot of nerve, but can also be a lot of fun, particularly when you're with friends. Good communication skills help keep you safe by helping you learn to say no and have people believe you. The following exercises will help you learn to use your voice effectively.

Exercise 1

Have a screamer. When you are in the loving presence of a group of supportive friends, you might want to stage a screamer. At a screamer all of you yell whatever you want at the top of your lungs. Since everyone is yelling at once, no one can really hear any one individual. You'll be amazed at the gutteral tones and sometimes profane words that come out of your mouth. Don't be embarrassed. Rape and sexual assaults are ugly matters of life, and they elicit a primitive response from us.

Exercise 2

Write it out. Some people can communicate better by writing than by speaking. I am not suggesting that you write notes or signs to your attacker, but writing might help you sort through issues of limits and boundaries better.

Begin with a general statement.

When I go out on a date I expect (to have a good time, to begin a meaningful relationship, to have an intellectually stimulating conversation—whatever you expect or wish from a date. Sometimes this will differ, depending on who your date is).

Then get more specific, particularly with regard to what you expect sexually from a date and the limits you would like to put on yourself as far as your own sexuality. Think about these issues carefully, and make wise judgments. Stick to them, and fight for them if necessary.

When I go out on a date I expect _____

_____

_____

_____

_____

I will set the following limits for myself. I will _____

_____

_____

_____

_____

I will not _____

_____

_____

_____

_____

10

How to Out-maneuver Rather Than Outmuscle an Attacker

A woman's response to a sexual attack depends on many things. Pauline B. Bart and Patricia O'Brien, with a grant from the National Institute of Mental Health, found that a woman's response to an attack may depend on such factors as upbringing (being taught to be feminine or to be "a lady"), height, birth position in the family, and knowledge of such survival skills as self-defense, first aid, or fire prevention.

Tall women might respond physically, while a woman who had many younger siblings might respond by speaking assertively and giving orders. A woman who was taught to be a "lady" at all times might try to talk her way out of an attack. A woman well versed in survival skills and accustomed to taking care of herself may use a common object as a weapon to defend herself.

Whatever works is a successful self-defense strategy. We cannot rely on any single response to protect ourselves from attack. We must learn to respond in various ways.

"Woman must not depend on the protection of man but must be taught to defend herself."—Susan B. Anthony, 1871

By far the most successful methods of avoiding rape involve using many different strategies. Bart and O'Brien said, "One of the most important findings was that *when a woman used physical force as a defense technique together with another technique, her chances of avoiding rape increased. In fact, the more additional strategies she used, the greater her chances.*

In other words, don't put all your eggs in one basket. If one approach doesn't work, try something else.

It is similar to doing an eye strike. If you use only one finger, you might miss. If you use two fingers, you double your chances of hitting the eyes. If you use three, or four, or all five fingers, then you increase your chances even more.

There are an infinite number of ways in which we can respond to an attack. The primary goal in all of these is to reduce the threat of violence to ourselves. We will do whatever it takes and use whatever skills necessary to keep ourselves safe and whole.

Although we can change our attitude, determination, and commitment to enhance our chances of staying safe, we must learn to deal with certain unalterable facts. One of these is that *men are generally physically stronger than women.* Not all men, of course, and not all women, but taken as a whole, men are usually bigger and stronger than we are.

In protecting ourselves, this means we need to learn to outmaneuver rather than outmuscle an attacker.

Often it is possible to thwart an attempted sexual assault without using violence. Because we know that rape is a crime of power rather than a crime of passion, we need to learn to use this knowledge to our advantage.

Although your best and safest defense may be not to fight back physically, it is important that you appear as if you could fight and win if you need to. *An air of confidence and personal power is the greatest defense you have against an attacker.* You must look like you are in control, even if you are in the grip of panic.

Fake it till you make it.

This air of confidence may be pure play acting on our part, but playing the strong, invincible woman may be the part that saves our lives.

Many tricks, maneuvers, and verbal responses have worked successfully against an attacker. Also, over and over again some nonphysical responses have proved to be ineffective.

What Did *Not* work:

- struggling (as opposed to focused resistance)
- arguing
- begging and pleading
- crying
- whimpering
- reasoning
- ignoring
- trying to please

Although many responses have been proved ineffective in stopping a rape, many more strategies are known to increase a woman's chance of getting to safety.

> **"When they were asked what strategies would be *ineffective* in avoiding a rape once accosted, the largest group said being passive or submitting, the second largest group said pleading . . ."—Pauline B. Bart and Patricia H. O'Brien** *Stopping Rape*

Successful Defense Strategies

- running away
- causing a scene by yelling, screaming, or using a whistle
- verbal responses that stall the attacker or buy more time
- assertive verbal responses that let the attacker know he chose the wrong woman
- using physical force

The single most successful rape avoidance strategy is running away. It will not work in all circumstances, of course. Sometimes escape is impossible. But where possible, an immediate exit seems to be a very smart thing to do.

Several considerations keep some women from fleeing immediately. Some women view flight as an admission of defeat, particularly when they are attacked at home. Other women are so intimidated by the circumstances they are unable to assert themselves enough to run.

For instance, if a man comes up to you while you are waiting for a bus or train and tells you not to move or make a sound, many of us will obey him because we have been taught to respect an authoritative voice. It is so ingrained in us to follow orders or to try to please those around us—even a stranger—that we have a difficult time recognizing the possibility of asserting ourselves.

Still other women are unable to run away because they are frozen with fear. The best way to combat this reaction is to admit rape and sexual assaults *can* happen, even to you. You may do everything right. You may go to the right places and take the best precautions, but you still may be attacked. Know that it can happen, and know that you can influence the situation if it does happen. Visualize yourself in the midst of an attack, successfully thwarting his attempts, then running to lights and safety.

Learn to create a moment of sheer bedlam by doing several self-defense strategies at once. Yell authoritatively ("Get out of my face!"), tell your attacker in no uncertain terms that he messed with the wrong woman, execute a focused eye strike and then a swift kick to the knee, and then run away to the safety of lights and people.

All of these tactics—yelling, asserting yourself verbally, kicks and strikes, then running away—done with the self-righteous fury of an attacked woman will undoubtedly affect the attacker. There are still no guarantees. He still may come after you. But by using more than one strategy, you have greatly increased your chances of avoiding rape.

Using What He Fears

We can enhance our chances for safety by exploiting an attacker's fears. Never assume that your attacker is invincible, for you are not the only one who is afraid during an attack.

What an assailant fears:

- failure
- pain
- getting caught
- loss of control
- being punished

According to Susan Smith's book, *Fear or Freedom,* "The attacker needs time, a relatively safe place to carry out the assault, and a victim who is sufficiently under his control." Most attackers fear the loss of any one of these factors. By taking control of any of them, we can increase our chances of safety.

Time

Time is the issue most often used by the victim. When attacked, you need to use time to your greatest benefit. To an attacker, any kind of delay indicates a loss of control of the situation. Because of this, most rapes are premeditated, with the crime, place, and usually the victim planned ahead of time and the attack carried through when the opportunity presents itself. Whenever the intended victim can throw the time schedule off, the attacker becomes increasingly nervous that he is losing control.

The best way to buy time is not to react according to his script. If he expects you to beg and plead, react strongly and assertively. If he expects you to go with him quietly and meekly, make as much noise and commotion as you can.

Buying time does not mean you simply stand there and don't react. You need to act immediately by assessing the situation and choosing the most appropriate response. You may choose to respond verbally or psychologically first, rather than physically.

> The best way to buy time is not to react according to his script.

The voice is a powerful weapon, particularly when effective words are used with strong, full-volumed noise. In buying time to get away to safety, figure out exactly what you want and express it to your attacker as clearly as possible and as often as is necessary.

Some case studies have indicated that women who repeat themselves over and over have finally convinced (or irritated) their attackers to let them go.

One woman who was attacked on the street immediately responded by saying, "My husband is expecting me, I've got to go home." At first the attacker ignored her, but she kept saying this over and over—not angrily or even aggressively, but persistently—until finally the attacker shouted at her, "Then go on home," and left.

Often an attacker will test out a potential victim by asking her a question or perhaps abusing her verbally by making rude or insinuating comments. If the woman appears intimidated or frightened, the situation may escalate into a full-powered sexual attack.

If an attack begins with verbal abuse or testing, you still want to take control. At this point, you may choose to respond strongly verbally rather than physically.

No matter how you respond to an attack, you must take immediate and unquestioned control of the situation.

If someone tries to stop you on the street—whether you are walking or in a car—*do not stop!* Never allow a stranger to come to the car window. If it is someone you believe needs help, go to the nearest safe spot and report the situation to the police.

Women have come up with innovative, creative, and sometimes humorous ways of thwarting an attack.

One woman who was grabbed on a deserted street pretended to go crazy. She kept saying she was hungry and then finally dropped to the ground beside the street and began eating the grass. Her attacker had no idea how to respond. She stalled long enough that he finally fled in surprise and disgust.

Women are particularly adept at verbal responses; we are taught from an early age how to use words to get what we want. What we want when facing a surprise attack is more time. The longer you can delay a stranger rape, the greater the chances of someone coming to your rescue.

Location

Where you are is also a factor in rape. Ideally, the attacker needs a secluded location to carry out the assault. *Never go willingly with an attacker to a remote area.* If a gun is involved, you may not have any option to going along, but you should fight hard not to get in a car with an attacker or to go with him to an abandoned or secluded spot.

The vast majority of rapes are committed in a car or a residence.

In the case of date rape, an isolated spot is almost always a factor. Scott Lindquist reports in his book, *Before He Takes You Out,* that an isolated spot, combined with alcohol, drugs, and criminal intent by the man almost always spells trouble. Places to avoid: empty dorm or fraternity house rooms, a car on a deserted road, vacation homes far from other houses, any place where there are no witnesses and people will be too far away to hear you.

Control

One defensive move that has seemed to work many times over is to trick an assailant into thinking that you are going along with him. Once you have convinced the attacker, he will often let down his guard, allowing you to strike quickly with force and power, then run to safety.

In a situation of stranger rape, this means allowing him to lead or push you a few steps before you retaliate. In an acquaintance rape, this may mean pretending to go along with him until you have an opportunity to escape. In the case of date rape, often the assailant will constrain the victim with only the weight of his body.

If he gets you on a bed or other flat surface, pretend to go along until you can roll on top of him and strike to the face or groin, or until you can create distance between you that may give you enough time to run if help is nearby.

Being convincing is everything when you are defending yourself. If you pretend to go along with an attacker, you might say something like, "Of course I want to make love to you. Just let me go freshen up first." Make sure he believes you so he will let you go, even for an instant. Once free of his grasp, either attack physically if the situation demands it or run like the wind if you can get away.

Another frequently used defensive tactic is to fake a medical problem of some sort. You might pretend to faint, to have a heart attack, or an epileptic attack.

There are advantages and disadvantages to this sort of response. The advantage is that you may be able to scare off an attacker without using force or violence. The disadvantage is that if you fall to the ground, it is more difficult to get up and run to safety if the opportunity arises. Another disadvantage is that your attacker may not be convinced and may kick you until you respond. Even if you really do faint, this is no guarantee that your attacker will leave you alone. He may just grab you by your hair and drag you to an isolated spot.

Perhaps the greatest danger in responding with a fake attack is that if it does not work, you will have difficulty regaining control of the situation. For instance, if you pretend to faint, you will have a hard time convincing your attacker that you are fearless and in control.

Ellen never saw him coming. She had worked late grading papers at school, and by the time she finished it was nearly dusk. As she hurried down the sidewalk in front of the school building, one of the maintenance men suddenly appeared from the alley, grabbing her arm from behind and pulling her toward him.

"I've been waiting for you, Ellen. I've been watching you for weeks having fun with all those little kids. Now you're going to have some fun with me," he growled in her ear.

Ellen's heart pounded, and for a moment she was so scared she thought that she was going to pass out.

The man kept pulling at her. "Come on."

Suddenly Ellen turned to him, put her best smile on, and dropped her books and papers. "I've been watching you, too. Come on, let's do it right here!" and she began to pull down her skirt.

For a moment the man stood staring at her. He finally said, "No, come on. Let's at least go back into the alley."

Ellen shook her head. "No, I'm not going back into that dirty old alley. It's here or nowhere."

Glancing around nervously, the man finally started backing

off. "Well, maybe later, Ellen," he mumbled before running away.

Ellen straightened her clothes, returned to the school building, and reported the attack to the school officials and the police. The maintenance man was caught that very evening.

Just as you are afraid that your attacker may be crazy, he fears that you may be crazy, too. Doing things totally out of the ordinary may help convince an attacker that he has chosen someone more unbalanced than himself. Several success stories have been told by women who have avoided an attack by acting crazy. Often their assailants have run off, shouting at them, "You're sick! You're crazy!" Interesting phrases for a rapist to use.

"Turning Off" an Attacker

Many women have reported that acting gross or disgusting or making themselves appear unclean or diseased has sometimes worked in thwarting an attack. Some women have told an attacker that they have AIDS or other sexually transmitted diseases, or that they are menstruating. Other kinds of behavior include:

- urinating
- farting
- vomiting
- burping
- defecating

These tactics probably work better in a date rape situation than a stranger rape. However, don't depend on any of these to save your life. To use them effectively, you need to be able to perform them on call. You might feel so scared that you think you are going to throw up, but can you really do it? You might be scared shitless, but can you control your bowel movements well enough to deliver?

The most effective use of gross behavior is in convincing a date that he is not seducing you. Even if you say No over and over again, he may be stuck in his Neanderthal thinking that you really mean yes and may continue with the candlelight and roses routine. You must communicate to him any way possible that rape is not your idea of romance. If you feel that a subtle approach is better than direct communication, you might make yourself appear so unappealing that he will want to be rid of you quickly.

A sexual attack is not something to which you can close your eyes and hope it will go away. Nor can we afford to simply suffer through it, either. The threat of AIDS has pushed us to realize that we must defend ourselves and our bodies. Even if we survive the attack itself, a completed rape is a life-threatening crime because of AIDS.

We all would like to think we could avoid rape by talking to an attacker and perhaps humanizing the situation, getting him to see us as human beings. We would like to think that if only we could *talk* to these men and help them realize the evil they are doing, perhaps we could save ourselves and them as well.

We know that bullies sometimes act the way they do because they are so intimidating they rarely get honest feedback.

Many women have relied on their ability to "win over with love" to keep themselves safe. We simply cannot afford to do that today. We are not only fighting the crazies on the street, we are fighting hundreds of years of culture and heritage that view sex as a commodity and women as conquests or playthings.

Perhaps in another time or in another world we will not have to fight for our right of safety. But for here and now, we can only afford generosity toward strangers after first seeing to our own safety.

"The Rape Journal" by Dell Fitzgerald-Richards (1974)

. . . . i did not bring this man upon my self
he came in the night
with knife and mask
I did not invite him into my home or bed
and i have to live with it

to deal with it (oh and i do mean that literally
oh so literally)
deal with it
every day at least once . . .

i hope that it warns you my luckier sisters
that you will be careful
both night and both day
and be alert
because we are at war even though
we are not ready and
we have not chosen this
not yet at any rate
and i hope that helps you
my other sisters
who have shared my experience . . .
that it will fire your anger
make you learn to fight back and kick and claw
hate even when necessary
more so to know
and be ready for that necessity
perhaps even learn to use knives and guns
but at least your own body
to protect yourself
for i love you my sisters
and we have been playthings too long.

—Oakland, California, Women's Press Collective

IN A NUTSHELL

1. Many factors influence a woman's response to an attack. These include upbringing, height, birth position in the family, role models she had as a child, and knowledge of basic survival skills.
2. The most successful methods of avoiding sexual attack involve using a physical defense together with another technique such as speaking assertively, yelling, and running.

3. The primary goal of successful self-defense is to lessen the chances of violence to ourselves.
4. We must learn to outmaneuver rather than outmuscle an attacker.
5. An air of confidence and personal power is the greatest defense we have against an attacker.
6. Strategies that do *not* work: begging, pleading, struggling, arguing, crying, whimpering, reasoning, ignoring, trying to please.
7. Self-defense strategies that *do* work: running away, causing a scene by yelling, blowing a whistle, stalling the attacker, assertive verbal responses, physical force.
8. The single most successful self-defense strategy is running away.
9. An assailant fears failure, pain, getting caught, loss of control, being punished.
10. We can influence the three things a rapist needs: time, place, and control of a victim.
11. No matter how we respond to an attack, we must take immediate and unquestioned control of the situation.
12. Never go willingly with an attacker to a remote area.
13. It is tragic that in our society we can only afford kindness to strangers after first seeing to our own safety.

Note: Learning basic survival skills will help us connect with ourselves at a very primitive level. Although we may never really need to know how to start a fire with one match, find water in the wilderness, or survive a snowstorm in the mountains, knowing that we have these skills will make us feel stronger and more capable. Learning basic survival skills is both empowering and fun.

Being able to execute many different self-defense strategies simultaneously should present little problem to most women. After all, if we can simultaneously cook dinner, help the kids with their homework, talk to the neighbor on the phone, and feed the dog, what could be so hard about kicking, yelling, arguing, and running all at the same time?

Exercise 1

Learn a variety of survival skills. Take a Red Cross first aid course. Read a book on safety in the home. Go to a camping and outdoors store and ask if they have any seminars on wilderness survival. You may never need to know how to start a fire, get water in the desert, or survive a snowstorm in the mountains, but knowing these skills will empower you.

Exercise 2

Create a minute of sheer bedlam.

Find a quiet, safe spot—your bedroom or bathroom or a friend's house will do. Pretend that you have been accosted on the street. For one minute yell, scream, cuss, kick, hit, strike, jump up and down, and anything else you can think of to do to create bedlam. Don't try to restrict what you say or do; let it all come out. One minute is a long time to sustain this kind of intensity. After a few seconds, your assailant would probably be halfway down the street.

After you are through and have visualized your attacker cringing in fear and running away as fast as he can, brush your hands off and give yourself a thumbs up sign for a job well done.

Exercise 3

Buy the loudest whistle you can find. Go to a park and use it. Have fun with it, and then put it on your key chain.

11

Fighting Back

Sometimes even if you do all the right things and avoid all the wrong places and wrong people, you may still find yourself in a perilous situation. Can you fight back?

Each one of us has the strength and potential to hurt someone. You have the capacity to inflict pain. Can you use it to defend yourself?

Self-defense is all about making choices. Physical retaliation increases your choices when you are in a dangerous situation. Responding physically is certainly not your only choice. You can talk to your attacker; you can try to divert his attention; you can act crazy; you can try to outrun him. But sometimes a physical response is the only one that will save you.

When someone attacks you physically, he has given up his right to fair play. When our basic rights are violated, we have the right to defend ourselves to regain safety, privacy, and peace of mind. No one has the right to hurt or victimize us.

By attacking you, an attacker has broken rules of culture and humanity. Although we may like to think of ourselves as non-violent and above a physical retaliation, we need to remember that we are not the ones who initiated the attack.

Many women believe they are not strong enough to fight back. *The issue is not one of strength but one of willingness to use the strength we already possess.* When I taught my first self-defense seminar to women, I was very pleased with the class and happy that my students had learned so many useful skills. As we were leaving after the last session, I was talking to the students about the course and they were very enthusiastic. I felt great until one girl said, "This was a lot of fun, but I don't think I'd ever be able to really hurt someone."

I looked at her in amazement and then looked at the rest of my students. "How about it? Could you use the techniques that you learned in this seminar?"

> When someone attacks you physically, he has given up his right to fair play.

They all looked at me. Most nodded yes, but a disturbing number of them shrugged their shoulders as if they never had really considered the possibility. I realized then that without this willingness to use what they had learned, the self-defense techniques I had taught them were essentially meaningless.

Unless you are willing to accept the fact that to defend yourself you might have to hurt someone, no amount of training and no number of tricks and self-defense techniques will do you the slightest good.

This is an inner issue that you must wrestle with on your own and a question you have to answer to yourself—before an attack happens. If you wait until you are actually in a dangerous situation, it will be too late. There will be no time for psychological thoughts in the midst of an attack. Each millisecond you hesitate is valuable time lost.

Most of us have never even thought of fighting physically. It is a concept fairly alien to how we were raised and what we feel comfortable doing.

Suppose you have led a relatively sheltered existence all of your life. The few times you have felt a little uncomfortable or slightly threatened by anyone, your father, brother, or boyfriend was always there to look after you. You naturally stepped aside and let one of them handle it. It made you feel safe, protected, and cherished to be able to let someone look after you and make sure you were not harmed.

"Being self-righteously non-violent when we see no other option is practicing passivism, more than pacifism. Increasing one's options for self-protection does not contribute to the violence; permitting oneself to be violated allows the violence to exist."—Frederique Delacoste and Fellice Newman, *Fighting Back: Feminist Resistance to Violence*

But what happens when Daddy is not there, your brother is away at college, and your new boyfriend turns out to have an aggressive mean streak in him and suddenly you are faced—all by yourself—with the possibility of being raped? The boyfriend is out of control, telling you that you are a cold little bitch and that it will be good for someone like him to show you what real men want. What are you going to do?

What are you going to do if you are a single parent trying to make ends meet and your boss keeps cornering you in the conference room, grabbing at you and telling you he knows you "want it"? What are you going to do if you've spent your entire life hating violence and working toward resolving conflicts and suddenly a man on the street pushes you back toward your car, telling you to take him to an isolated part of town?

What are you going to do? This is when you will find out things about yourself that you never knew. The need for survival pulls out our strongest instincts. This is when you dig deep and find out exactly who and what you are. No one really wants to fight, but how much can we put up with? Is there anything that we can do?

We *can* do something. We *all* can do something. We can fight back. We can fight verbally; we can fight psychologically; we can fight politically; and we may even need to fight physically.

By standing up for ourselves and by fighting back when it is necessary, we will begin to put out a clear message: we will not be victims any longer.

Fighting back physically when attacked is an honorable

choice. Sometimes, when danger is very close, it is the only choice we have to save ourselves.

The kind of courage we need to fight back is one, perhaps, we have never needed before. Men have all kinds of terms for digging deep and showing courage. We all hear statements like, "It's where they separate the men from the boys; it takes real balls to stand up for your rights; you have to be a real man about it."

But women are so unused to standing up for ourselves and showing physical courage, we do not even have any corresponding descriptions. "It's where we separate the girls from the women? It takes real ovaries? Be a real woman?" They sound strange right now, but who knows? They just might catch on.

Taking Control

When in a potentially dangerous position, take a deep breath and assess the amount of danger you face.

The first sign that you are faced with danger may be someone invading your physical space. If a man sits next to you on public transportation when plenty of other seats are available, be on your guard.

If your date insists that you sit close to him or puts his hand on your thigh, making you uncomfortable, be wary.

The degree of danger you are facing also depends on where you are. If you are close to safety, then your level of danger is not extreme. If you are at an abandoned beach miles from the nearest telephone and your date begins to get heavy hands, your level of danger is considerably greater.

If you are in a relatively low-risk situation, you do not want it to escalate. You must do everything you can to halt the danger. You must communicate directly and clearly. At this juncture there can be no misunderstandings.

If a stranger is making you feel uncomfortable, you need to take stock of your options. Change seats if you need to. If he is staring at your body parts and several people are around, go ahead and embarrass him by telling him you find it horribly offensive to be stared at.

You might want to start shouting for an imaginary friend if someone starts to bug you. Don't just use any name. "Bubba" is much more effective than "Harold."

If a date or an acquaintance is making you feel a little scared, let him know immediately that you are in control of the situation and that you mean business.

If you request that he move his hand and he ignores you or doesn't understand that you really mean it, pinch him hard in the stomach, inner thigh, or anywhere else you can reach easily. Other options are tweaking his nose, twisting his ear, or pulling his hair. These are relatively painful, but certainly not life-threatening, techniques for getting his attention. They are also a little embarrassing, and he probably will not argue with you. At this point he doesn't want to cause a scene. What is he going to do? Jump up and tell his fraternity brothers that you pinched him? If he has any sense at all, he will back off. If he does not, you are going to need a stronger response.

Fighting Back Physically

When you are faced with a *real* threat of being raped or are in danger for your life, you need to respond in a way that will get you to safety as quickly as possible.

In spite of a clear and present danger, many women hesitate to fight back physically. One of the most serious stumbling blocks preventing women from defending themselves is the myth that fighting back is the wrong thing to do. Many women believe that if they resist, they will enrage the attacker, making things worse. Many other women believe there is no point in fighting back because they would never be able to break away from a bigger, stronger attacker.

Experts and statistics negate these myths.

Women who resist (by kicking, screaming, talking, arguing, running, or any other means) have a fifty-fifty chance of stopping the attack. According to the Los Angeles Commission on Assaults Against Women, *if a woman has participated in self-defense training, then she increases her chances of stopping an attack to 75 percent.*

This training does not need to involve years of karate or

A study funded by the National Mental Health Institute reports that women who responded physically had a better chance of avoiding rape. There seemed to be no relationship between a woman's fighting back physically and increased physical injury to her body over and above the rape. Further, the study found that sexual assault usually does not result in serious physical injury. Resisting usually resulted in minor injuries such as scratches and bruises.

combat instruction. The most effective physical self-defense moves are those which are learned quickly and which you remember easily. These moves are designed to cause the greatest amount of pain in the least amount of time, allowing you to escape and run for help.

There are no guarantees that fighting back will result in your getting away unharmed. Sometimes fighting back does cause an attacker to become more violent. Far more often, however, fighting back with fierce determination allows a woman to get away. *Your primary objective in fighting back is to hit hard and fast and run toward lights, people, and safety, thus avoiding rape and injury to yourself.*

Are you strong enough to stop an attack? There's never an unqualified answer to this question. When a beauty pageant contestant went to prize fighter Mike Tyson's hotel room, she must have known that she would be totally helpless on a physical level.

But, luckily, few men are as strong or as highly trained as Mike Tyson, and fortunately most women are much stronger than they give themselves credit for being. It does not take the strength of a Mike Tyson to defend yourself. You just need to know where and when to strike and with what. *Self-defense is not a sporting event. It is survival at the most primitive level, and there are no rules.*

The amount of force you use to defend yourself depends on the amount of force or threat of force used against you. For instance, if a

> **Robin Warshaw wrote of a young college woman in her book *I Never Called It Rape,* "I felt raped, but I didn't realize I had been raped. . . . It didn't occur to me that it was okay to hurt him, to kick him in the balls, or punch him in the eye. Good girls don't do that. You sort of just lie back and let this happen, and then you deal with the consequences."**

man comes up to you in a bar and says, "Hey baby, looking pretty good tonight. Want to go out?" and touches your arm suggestively, you cannot retaliate by turning around and breaking his knee cap.

Although you may not like it if someone you do not know touches you (and rightly so!), the amount of force and even threatened force in this situation is minimal and requires a minimal response. A strong, "No, go away and leave me alone!" would probably be a sufficient and appropriate self-defense move.

If at this point he tightens his hold on your arm, pulls you toward him, and says, "You're coming with me whether you like it or not," the amount of force has escalated and a stronger response from you is necessary and appropriate.

Never underestimate your strength. It takes little power to dislocate a knee and render an attacker incapable of following you until you reach safety. Only five pounds of pressure can rupture an eardrum and one and one-half pounds of pressure can dislocate a finger.

> **Not fighting back is a result of years of cultural training and conditioning. Girls simply are not expected to fight. Sadly, it is often easier for women to receive pain than it is for them to inflict it.**

In addition to actually helping to stop an attack, fighting back has other benefits. Those women who chose to fight back when assaulted are thought to have recovered psychologically 50 percent faster than those women who did not.

"Some women have said that resisting the attack in every way possible made them feel better about themselves afterward . . . one of the most important functions of physical resistance is to keep women from feeling depressed even if they have been raped."—Pauline B. Bart and Patricia H. O'Brien, *Stopping Rape*

The key issue here is the feeling that these women felt themselves to have exerted some control or influence over events. They feel like survivors, not victims. *As long as we have some control over what happens, the victim mentality is greatly reduced.* Even if you choose to submit rather than fight back physically, you are making a conscious choice, rather than just being swept along with the events beyond your control. It is a viable and honorable choice under many circumstances.

Every situation will be different. Every assault presents a different challenge. It is absurd to think of trying to fight off Mike Tyson physically; it simply is an impractical choice for anyone I know, man or woman.

But it is both possible and highly practical to fight when attacked under most circumstances.

Fighting back takes a great deal of bravery. If you decide to fight, it must be a lightning-fast decision. You must strike with as much speed, intensity, power, and focus as you can possibly muster. There is no such thing as successful half-hearted physical self-defense. It is an all-or-nothing situation.

It is also important to realize the difference between struggling and fighting. The word *struggle* brings to mind a proper little lady beating her tiny fists against the chest of a big, strong man. This is not effective self-defense. Instead, imagine yourself walking down a city street and suddenly a man springs out from between two parked cars and grabs your arm, telling you to come with him. Without hesitating, you spin around, jab him in the eyes, and utter a guttural yell of anger and defiance. This causes him to release his hold on you. You then take charge of the situation. Grab his shoulder and, with astounding strength, strike his jaw with your elbow. His head snaps back, but you're not quite through. You raise your leg up high and kick forcefully to his knee, dislocating it. As he is writhing in pain and astonishment, you run faster to lights, people, and safety than you've ever run in your life. There you immediately dial 911 and report the assault to the police. That is effective self-defense.

> There is a vast difference between struggling and fighting.

Yes, you hurt him. But you are alive and whole to tell about it and report it to the police so he can be stopped from attacking other women who do not have the strength and fortitude you possess.

It really happens this way. Women are tired of being assaulted. At a very primitive level, we are tired of being picked on physically, and we will not stand for it any longer.

It is helpful to keep in mind that men, too, have been conditioned to expect a certain response. When you react with a different script, a rapist is momentarily disconcerted. Take advantage of this confusion. Strike hard and effectively, then get to safety.

When you choose to fight back, you are going to cause a scene. Good breeding and polite manners have their places, but a life-and-death situation on the street is not one of them. This is your *life,* and you will do whatever is necessary to survive.

It is easy to lose sight of our perspective, so practice keeping the big picture in mind. Try to visualize a worst case scenario. If you are in a boy's room at the fraternity house and he begins to maul you, one option is to stay quiet and not embarrass him. The result of this approach is probable rape, with the worry of pregnancy and AIDS. After all, if he's doing this to you, he's probably done it to other women, too.

The alternative? If you yell and fight back, you're going to make a scene. You might get laughed at and scorned by his friends. You might even get hit or beat up. But these are wounds that will heal. In choosing to fight back, you have decided to be a survivor rather than a victim. You have made a decision to keep yourself safe and alive.

"It is possible for a woman to fight off a man, but she needs to be prepared—practically and emotionally—for that possibility in adance."—Robin Warshaw, *I Never Called It Rape*

Weapons at Your Disposal

What you can use as a weapon is limited only by your imagination. Virtually any hard or sharp object can be used to hit an assailant. Many substances can be sprayed or thrown into an attacker's face to temporarily blind him.

When using makeshift weapons it is important to remember:

- They will only slow down an attacker. Be prepared to run.
- Whatever you use against an attacker, there is a chance that he can gain control and use it against you as well.

Your best use of a weapon is to pick up whatever you can get your hands on fastest. This will depend on where you are, what is lying around, or what you are carrying. Every situation will be different, but the following may give you some ideas:

- Your arms are full of grocery bags, and someone grabs your arm from behind and threatens you. Spin around and throw the bags in his face.

- You are at the kitchen sink. Someone breaks through the front door and comes into the kitchen, holding a big club. Take the pot of beef stew on the stove and throw it at his face. Grab the drain cleanser from under the sink and spray it in his eyes. Yank the toaster out of the wall, spin it by the long cord, and hit him in the temple.
- You are in your dorm room getting ready for bed. Suddenly the door opens and an obviously drunk freshman is lurching toward you, threatening to "get some." Grab your hair spray and spray it into his eyes. Take your tennis racket and hit him in the temple or across the nose.
- You've heard something outside. You grab a flashlight and are out investigating when you hear someone behind you. You spin around and an attacker is only inches away from you. Ram the flashlight up under his nose and thrust it upward.

There are countless ways to defend yourself with an innumerable number of items. Use your imagination. Use your ingenuity, but most of all, use your self-confidence and assertion to defend yourself as fully as necessary. Remember, when you are attacked, you want to make yourself as much of a pain as possible. Use whatever is available to you. Remember when your brother used to chase you around the house and you would run, screaming, slamming doors in his face, shoving chairs in his way, and throwing pillows or anything else you could get your hands on? Those same tactics are effective if you are being chased by an assailant. Make it as difficult as possible for him to get to you.

If you are outside, grab a handful of sand or dirt and throw it in his eyes. Inside, use whatever you can grab easily.

The greatest danger in using any kind of traditional weapon is in believing that it alone will keep you safe. For a weapon to do any good, you must be able to put your hands on it immediately and use it effectively.

Many woman carry mace in their purse and think they are safe against an attacker. *If* the woman has it in her hand when she is attacked, and *if* her arms are free, and *if* the spray works correctly, and *if* the chemicals have not gone bad, and *if* the assailant comes toward her head on, and *if* the wind is not blowing, and *if* the attacker is not intoxicated from drugs or alcohol, then mace is an effective deterrent.

Obviously, the usefulness of mace depends on many facts. The label on a can of mace points this out, as it reads, "Use extreme care with intoxicated, drugged, demented, enraged, or other persons having reduced sensitivity to pain and who may react with violence if not incapacitated with this weapon." In other words, it only works on sane, calm, sober people. Not a comforting thought.

> In fighting back, you want to go for the most vulnerable areas of an attacker with the strongest parts of your body.

Tear gas is another chemical weapon often used in self-defense. It can be sprayed from three to ten feet away; it wears off in thirty to forty-five minutes; and it can be used with an ultraviolet dye that marks the assailant. The disadvantage is that it has a shelf life of only six months. In other words, it should be ordered directly from the manufacturer and replaced in your purse every six months.

Of course, other more deadly weapons are available. Stun guns, handguns, knives, and clubs are all easily purchased in this country. If you decide to carry one of them, know that an attacker can wrestle then away from you and use them against you. If you choose to defend yourself with a deadly weapon, know how to handle it, practice with it regularly, and use it responsibly.

If you don't have anything to use as a weapon, you're going to have to use your body. All of us have very effective weapons on our bodies: hands, fingernails, feet, knees, elbows, heads, and brains. Your best weapon is your brain. Keep thinking. Try to figure out what he expects you to do, and do just the opposite.

In fighting back, you want to go for the most vulnerable areas of an attacker with the strongest parts of your body. In other words, you want to inflict the greatest amount of pain in the least amount of time with the least discomfort to yourself.

> **"Self-defense includes learning physical maneuvers, but it also involves an attitude. Self-defense is 10 percent technique and 90 percent intestinal fortitude. You have to have determination—the will to protect yourself."—Dan Lena and Marie Howard, *Sexual Assault: How to Defend Yourself.***

If you are attacked, take a deep breath, assess your situation, and choose the defense you feel is the best. Your adrenalin rush will soon change to an adrenalin dump, so act quickly and decisively.

Any technique you use to defend yourself will be even more effective if you yell loudly and fiercely while you are doing it. The voice is a powerful weapon. Even while you are practicing these techniques, yell *No!* as loudly as you can.

Like anything else, practice will increase your effectiveness. Each of the techniques listed below can be learned in a matter of a few minutes. Most will come to you naturally. Practicing them over and over will help them come more quickly for you if you ever need them.

Include a short one-minute self-defense routine in your daily habits. After you have washed your face and brushed your teeth, face the mirror and do a series of techniques. This will keep these defensive moves sharp and at your fingertips, and it will also be a daily reminder of the importance of protecting yourself. Use it as a ritual, symbolizing that you can take care of yourself. For the one-minute self-defense workout, see page 182.

> **Once an assailant has initiated an attack by grabbing you, touching you, or making it clear from his speech that he intends to harm you, he has given up his right to fair play. Once that line has been crossed, *you* will the situation. From then on, you are the one in control.**

It is impossible to practice full-powered self-defense moves with a partner. By definition, they are painful, sometimes debilitating moves that you only want to perform if your life is in danger. You can practice *at* a partner, but be careful not to make contact. The danger of injury is high.

If your husband or boyfriend wants to see what you've learned from "that self-defense book" or techniques you have picked up from a self-defense seminar, you can't really show him without hurting him. However, to get his attention, try this. Take the palm of your hand and push against his nose. He'll back up quickly. Now ask him if he wants you to do it full force!

Distracting Techniques

If you are grabbed, your first instinct will be to pull away from the attacker. If you try to outmuscle him, you will have difficulty getting away. Instead, execute what is commonly called a distracting technique. This is a quick technique that will effectively get the attacker's focus off of holding on to you. *Distracting techniques should be accompanied by a loud yell and must be followed up by other kicks or strikes that make it impossible for your attacker to follow you.* Sometimes an attacker is so surprised, disheartened, and fearful of your retaliation that a distracting technique is all that is necessary. But always be ready to do more if you need to.

Distracting Techniques

- **jab to the eyes**
- **palm heel strike to the nose**
- **jab to the throat**
- **scratch down face**
- **hammer fist to the temple or nose**
- **strike to the ears**

Eye Strike

Of all self-defense techniques *the best and most effective is a strike to the eyes*. Think about when you had an eyelash or piece of dirt in your eye and how painful it was. Now imagine someone's fingernails in your eyes. When struck in the eyes, the natural reaction is to raise both hands to the eyes, thus effectively releasing you. Many women say that they are squeamish about striking someone in the eyes. Get real! Think about the horror stories you have heard about rapists. Unless you rip out the eyeball, an eye will heal. It is a quick, painful defense that is highly effective.

Use all your fingers and bend them slightly to prevent jamming or breaking them on contact. Keeping your hand and elbow in the same plane, pull back your elbow and forcefully

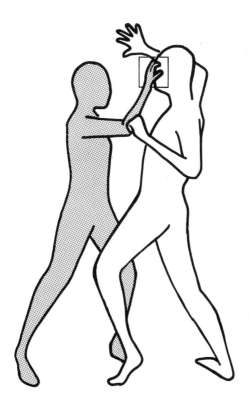

thrust your fingers forward while yelling *No!* If you only use a single finger, you might miss. Increase your chances of success five times over by using all the digits on one hand.

To practice the eye strike, use a soft plastic or paper plate. Hold the plate with one hand and practice striking it with your fingertips with the other. If it helps you visualize this defensive move, draw a pair of eyes on the plate.

Scratch to the Face

One natural weapon many women always carry is their long, sharp fingernails. If you have to defend yourself from close-in, this is an excellent defensive move. Picture a tiger getting ready to scratch, and your fingers will automatically go into the right position: hand taut, fingers taut. If possible, use both hands. You still should aim primarily at the eyes, but scratch all the way down the face with as much force as you can. Go up and down, or across and back, whatever comes most naturally to you and wherever you can reach the best, growling, hissing, or yelling during your defense.

To feel the force of this defense, gently scratch your own arm. Then imagine that force multiplied a hundred times over, which is what you are capable of in a moment of fear and anger.

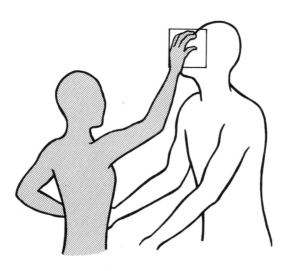

Palm Heel Strike

A palm heel strike to the nose is another effective weapon. Push on your own nose gently, and you can imagine immediately how much pain a full-force blow can cause.

Tilt your hand backward so the bottom of your palm almost, but not quite, faces the ceiling. Fold in your fingers. Be sure to keep the fingers out of the way so you will not break them. Pull the top of your palm back even with your shoulder, keeping your elbow in line with your palm, and thrust it forward, envisioning your palm hitting just under the nose, pushing it upward and yelling at the same time. Practice thrusting it forward over and over again until the motion feels comfortable to you. (Be careful that you do not overextend your elbow.) This is a powerful technique.

Practice the palm heel strike into a pillow. With one hand, hold a small pillow head level against a wall. With the other hand, execute a palm heel strike. Do not slap at the pillow. You should feel the force of your blow at the base of your palm. Yell.

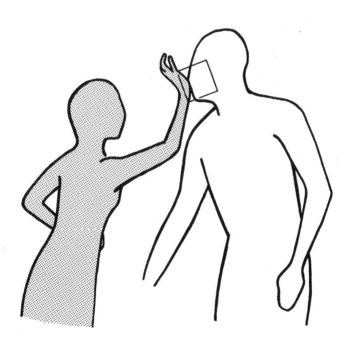

Punch to the Throat

It is usually not wise to punch with a fist unless you are trained to do so. The chances of breaking bones in your hand are too great. But the throat is a relatively soft—and highly effective—target.

Gently push on your own throat at the base of the windpipe. With minimum pressure you start to choke and lose your breath. Make a good tight fist and practice going toward an attacker's windpipe. Punch as hard as you can against a pillow for practice. Yell.

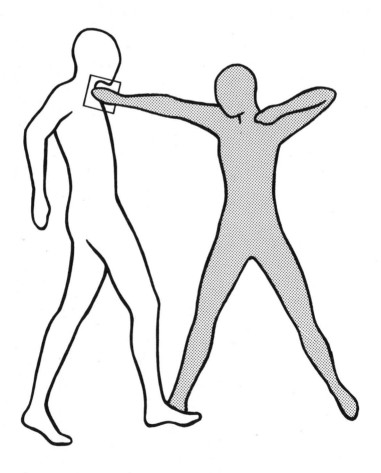

Hammer Fist to the Temple or Nose

Another safe closed-hand technique for a beginner is the hammer fist. Make a good, tight fist with your stronger hand, and then turn your palm downward. Now hit the fleshy side of your hand opposite your thumb. You're probably surprised at how hard and strong it feels. It *is* strong. Use it. Pull your hand high above your head and with as much strength as possible, come straight down on an attacker's nose or swing and hit the temple. Don't forget the yell.

This is a strong, effective technique, one worthy of practicing over and over until you feel comfortable with it. To practice, beat down on a bed or sofa.

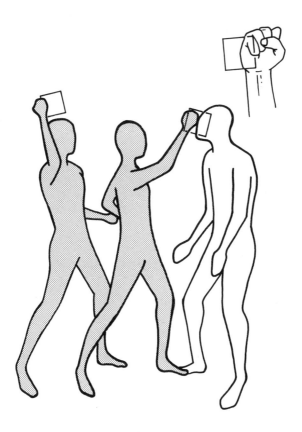

Blow to the Eardrums

If you have both hands free, cup your hands slightly and forcefully strike your attacker over the ears as if you are playing cymbals. This may cause a great deal of pain and may burst your attacker's eardrums.

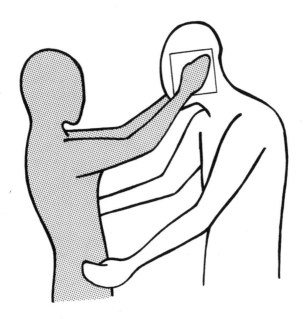

Don't Stop Too Soon

One of the worst things you can do is to initiate a strong defense, then stop too soon, assuming you have incapacitated your attacker when you have only momentarily deterred him.

You must follow up. You must stay in control of the situation until you are certain that you can escape to safety.

What you do to follow up in your defense will depend entirely on your situation. The most effective follow-through will be executed if you can control your attacker by grabbing his shoulder or clothing. Remember that at this point you are in control. You want the man close enough to damage him. If you grab him, this will keep him from moving or turning away from you, making your defensive techniques stronger. Even though the thought of touching him anywhere may be repulsive to you, it's important that you finish your defense as strongly as is humanly possible.

The strongest defensive weapons are the hardest parts of your own body: your feet, knees, and elbows. They should be used against the most vulnerable parts of your attacker's body: his jaw, solar plexus (the soft part of the stomach just below the center of the rib cage), groin, and knees.

If You Are Attacked from the Front

If the attacker grabs one arm or your clothing, immediately execute one of the distracting techniques. If he grabs both arms or hands, use your head to butt into his face, or go directly to a shin kick or kick to the instep.

After doing the distracting techniques, follow up with one of these techniques. Don't forget to yell.

Kick to the Knee

A well-executed kick to the knee has the double advantage of causing him much pain and making it difficult for your attacker to run after you. If you hit the knee area from the side or the back with full force, you can do serious damage. It is very easy to dislocate or break a knee joint.

Because you don't want to miss, again grab your attacker by the wrist or shoulder. This time you want to stomp downward on the side of the knee. Raise your knee as high as you can and, using a stomping motion, kick downward toward an imaginary knee. This is a much stronger kick than pulling your knee behind you and kicking upward.

Practice this kick over and over again. Find an old sofa that is approximately the same height as your knees and practice kicking it. Ideally you want to hit with your heel, the hardest part of your foot. Also practice kicking a little higher than the sofa, as your attacker probably will be a bit taller than you. Only practice this with a partner under the supervision of a trained self-defense instructor. You will be amazed at how much damage you can do with the slightest amount of pressure.

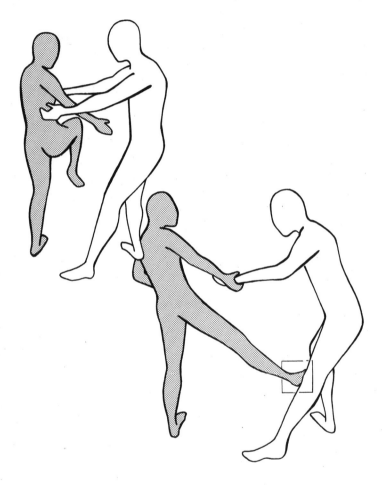

Knee Strike or Kick to the Groin

A blow to the groin has limited usefulness. If a man expects a self-defense move at all, he will probably expect it to come to the groin area. If you kick to the groin, make sure it is a fast snappy kick and that you recoil your foot immediately so he cannot grab the foot and throw you off balance.

Some attackers have become so savvy in their crimes that they actually wear groin cups under their clothing to protect this area.

However, the groin remains an area of extreme sensitivity in a man. If you are in close to an assailant, a knee to the groin is a powerful, effective technique to use. For greatest effect, grab his shoulder or the front of his coat and come in underneath the groin area. Pull him downward as you drive your lower thigh up as high as possible.

The groin area is a good target only if you can get to it easily. If you do not have a clear shot at it or if he has on tight pants or stands with his legs close together, choose another target.

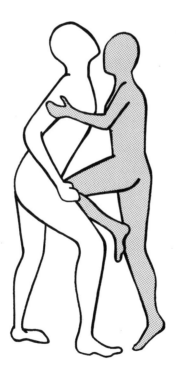

Grabbing the Hair

If you strike below the waist, your assailant's body may fall toward you. You need to be ready for this and take advantage of it. After a swift knee to the groin, your attacker will most probably double over in pain. This is a perfect opportunity to grab him by the hair of the head and execute a knee to the face or to the solar plexus.

Kick to the Shin

There are many nerve endings in the shin, and it is an area virtually unprotected by muscle or fat. Just pull your knee back and kick right to the shin with your toes, a move particularly effective in sharp-pointed shoes. Although this is a painful technique, it will only stop an assailant temporarily. He will still be able to run after you.

Elbow Strike to the Jaw or Ribs

Your elbow is one of the strongest bones in your body. With your hand, feel that nice, hard bone going down your lower arm. Now move your hand upward until you feel the point of your elbow. Look at the knuckles in your hand, and then look at your elbow. Just consider it a giant knuckle! It is a powerful weapon.

Turn your hand so the palm is facing down and make a good, tight fist. Keeping the fist and elbow in the same plane, cock your elbow back. With as much force as possible, strike across the jaw with the point of your elbow. To make this even more effective, hold on to his shoulder as you do this, pulling him into the strike. If your attacker is much taller than you are and you cannot reach his jaw, the same technique can be done to the solar plexus or ribs. If you are in close, bring your elbow up directly under his jaw. This can be practiced into a pillow.

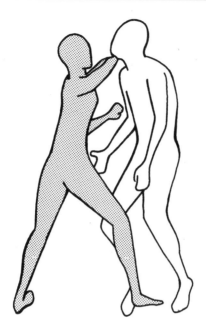

If You Are Attacked from the Rear

If someone attacks you from behind, you have an immediate psychological advantage. What a wimp! He doesn't even have enough nerve to attack from the front. He has to sneak up behind you. Remind yourself of this often.

If an Attacker Grabs One Arm from Behind

To release your attacker's grip, do not try to pull away. Spin around to face him, and execute one of the distracting techniques, preferably the eye strike, while yelling loudly. Chances are very good that after you have struck someone in the eye, throat, or nose, he will let go of you. If this is not the case, you need to release his grip.

The Thumb

When escaping from a grab, do a distracting technique and yell, then go for the weakest part of an attacker's hand. If you pull out of his grasp, pull toward his thumb. If he has hold of only one arm or wrist, clasp both your hands together and pull your arms sharply and quickly toward his thumb. Practice this with a partner until it is fairly easy for you to determine where the thumb is when you are grabbed.

The Little Finger

Another weak spot on an attacker's hand is his little finger. After you have done a softening technique and yelled "No!", grab your attacker's little fingers and bend them sideways hard. This is not the time to be squeamish. If your life or body is in danger, go ahead and break the finger. It will heal. You may not.

If the attacker grabs you around the neck from behind, *you must* release his hold as quickly as possible. It is only a matter of seconds before you will begin to black out from lack of oxygen. If he has you with his forearm across your throat, immediately turn your head into the crook of his arm. There will be a small pocket of room there, allowing you to catch your breath.

While yelling for help, kick to his shins as hard as you can, thrust your hips backward to throw him off balance, and immediately reach up and find his little fingers. Yank on them hard. Your life depends on it. Once he has released you—he will—spin around to face him and follow through. Anyone who has tried to choke you is a serious threat to your life. Do not hesitate to incapacitate him.

If your attacker wraps both arms around you, as in a bear hug, you still have weapons you can use. Your immediate softening technique should be to butt your head directly into his face while yelling loudly. If your attacker is a good deal taller than you, this will not work. It is senseless to beat your head against his chest. Thrust your hips back into his body, throwing him off balance, and kick to the knee to follow up. Yell!

If he actually picks you up off the ground in this position, you can still kick. Particularly if he is carrying you to a car or to a secluded spot, do everything you can. It is impossible for him to hold a hand over your mouth at this point, so be sure you scream and yell and curse and argue as loudly as you can.

Stomp to the Instep

As a follow-up (or an initial defense if your attacker is tall), raise your knee up high and stomp to his instep or the top of his foot. This is even more effective when you are wearing high-heeled shoes. Even more painful is to take your sharp high heel or the side of your shoe and scrape down the side of your attacker's leg while yelling, "No!"

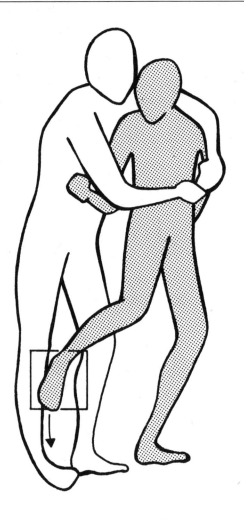

Scrape Down Leg

"We are what we repeatedly do. Excellence, then, is not an act, but a habit."—Aristotle

Elbow to the Ribs

If your attacker has grabbed you by the shoulders or upper arms, immediately reach forward as if you are grabbing a handful of air, palm upward. Close your hand, making a fist, and with all your strength, ram your elbow into his ribs or solar plexus, keeping the palm up so that you hit with the point of your elbow. As you hit, give a good, loud yell. As he releases you, turn toward him, grab his shoulder, and follow up with a hard kick to the side of the knee.

Slap/Squeeze to the Groin

If a man's testicles are forcibly squeezed for a count of eight seconds, he will be in so much pain he will be incapable of retaliating. If you do this, make sure you grab the testicles, not the penis. If you are grabbed from behind, either slap with an open hand or punch with your fist to the groin area. Immediately grab the testicles and twist them like you are taking the lid off a jar. Squeeze hard for a slow count to eight. Don't be squeamish here. Grab hard, dig your fingernails in, twist, and hold on. If an assailant is wearing tight pants, this technique will not work.

If you are in a rape position and the assailant insists that you touch his genitals, this is an *excellent* defensive move.

If You Are Knocked to the Ground

As quickly as possible roll to your back and draw up with your arms and knees in close to your body, hands and feet ready to defend yourself. As your attacker comes in closer, kick out hard to the knee, or to the shin and yell, "No!" Keep your arms extended, hands in tight fists to keep him away.

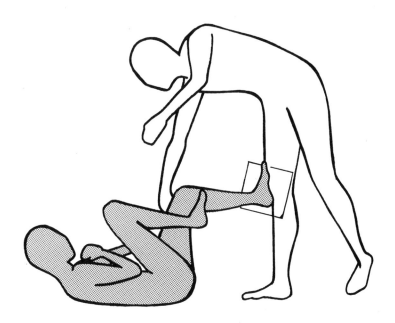

If You Are in Imminent Danger of Being Raped

A rapist cannot complete a sexual act while holding on to you with both hands. At some point he has to let go so he can get to his pants or yours. The moment there is a shift in his position, you strike as hard as possible.

If the rapist demands that you touch his genitals, use this moment to grab, jerk down, squeeze hard, and yell loudly.

Fight hard to avoid being flat on your back straddled by a

potential rapist who has both arms pinned. If you are caught by surprise or if he somehow gets you into this position, you are still not helpless. Wait for the best moment to make your defensive moves. Remember, he has to change his position at some point. A knee rammed into the groin or thrusting upward is effective, but it may throw his body on top of yours. Be ready to move quickly. This is a particularly good move if there is a wall or headboard in back of you so that he hits his head as he pitches forward.

Defense Against Weapons

It is a dangerous time to be a woman in America. We have a greater chance of being a victim of violent crime than we do of being hurt in a traffic accident.

At no other time in our history has it been more important for us to learn to take responsibility for our own safety and well-being.

"In the last fifteen years, violent crimes against women have increased by 50 percent. Meanwhile, violent crimes against men have decreased by 12 percent."—National Organization of Women, October 1990

The same fundamental rules used against an unarmed assailant are basic to self-defense against an attacker with a weapon. It is still important for us to:

- take a deep breath;
- assess the danger of the situation;
- respond with multiple strategies (run, yell, fight back, argue, cause a scene).

If the assailant has a weapon, the danger escalates dramatically. This does not mean that we are helpless against a weapon.

If He Has a Knife

Whenever an attacker uses a weapon, he must feel he cannot control the situation without one. This should give the victim an immediate psychological advantage.

When defending against a knife, realize there is a fair chance you will be cut, but also know that knife cuts are rarely lethal. Unless the knife goes directly into a vital organ or severs an artery, you will not die from a knife wound. If you prepare yourself ahead of time for the probability of being cut, you will not go into shock if it actually happens. Think about the victims who have been stabbed dozens of time and survived the attack. The greatest danger from a knife attack is multiple stabbings and loss of blood.

Positioning plays an extraordinarily important role when defending against a knife. If an attacker is several feet away from you, *do not get any closer. Do not get into a car with him.* Take control of the situation, and do not let him intimidate you. Run away as quickly as you possibly can, yelling for help. You must escape before he gets close enough to use the knife.

Many women are scared to do this, believing that he may throw the knife. Chances of this happening are slight. Even if he does throw it, it probably will not penetrate very deeply.

If he is in close enough to cut you with the knife, you will have to make some hard, fast decisions. You can guess a lot about how experienced an attacker is by noticing the kind of knife he uses. If he is holding a pocket knife or a kitchen knife, he is probably inexperienced.

No matter what kind of knife it is, if an attacker has a knife to your throat, do not move. Do exactly as he says.

Remember, though, it is almost impossible for him to rape you while he holds a knife to your throat.

With a knife to your throat, your best defense is generally a psychological one. Talk to him. Do not plead or beg, but pretend to go along with what he says. Once he feels confident, he may put down the weapon.

As soon as he removes the knife from your neck, make your move, quickly and without hesitation.

Do not try to wrestle with your attacker over control of the knife at first. Bypass the knife and go straight for one of the strongest retaliations you are capable of. A man with a knife is clearly a strong threat to your life. Remove the immediate threat as quickly as possible.

If you are in close, go for the testicles. Twist, yank down hard, and squeeze for a slow count of eight while yelling as loudly as you can. Remember that a man will be in such shock and pain during these eight seconds he will likely pass out or at least go limp. He cannot struggle during this time for any movement will only increase the pain.

"Never signal your intentions. Think fast and wait for or create the opportunity to escape."—Susan Smith, *Fear or Freedom*

If He Has a Gun

If your attacker has a gun, all the rules are changed. You cannot outsmart or outrun a bullet. Your immediate question will be, Is it loaded? Assume it is. Only you can assess your situation here. But remember that a 1986 study found that when the rapist carried a gun, the targeted victim was able to fight off the attack 51 percent of the time.

If a man pulls up in a car, points a gun at your face, and tells you to get inside, you are faced with one of the toughest decisions of your life. If you turn and run, he may shoot you. If you comply, he may shoot you anyway. This is a very personal decision. If the attacker is insane enough to shoot you in the back, he is probably a sadistic madman who would not stop with rape. While you still have a fifty–fifty chance to run to safety, most self-defense experts would urge you to take this chance.

You are not helpless when faced with a gun, but your tactics will have to be different. Each of us will have to make our own judgments about how we defend ourselves. *Often, when a gun is involved, the only sure defense is to submit to the attack. This is an honorable choice. If you live through the attack, then you have made a good choice.*

Victims are shot less than 4 percent in all victimizations.—U.S. Department of Justice, 1990

The Basic Rules for Fighting Back Physically

- Take a deep breath and control your panic.
- Decide immediately the level of danger you are in and respond appropriately.
- Yell!
- Yell again as you execute a distracting technique and take control.
- Follow up with as many strong techniques as are needed to incapacitate the attacker. Yell.
- Run as fast as you can to lights, safety, and people.
- Report the attack to the authorities.
- Don't underestimate the effect of the attack, even if you are physically unhurt. Talk to friends or a counselor. Take care of yourself.

When defending yourself physically against an attacker, you have the tremendous advantage of determination and commitment. Do not hesitate to defend yourself with as much strength and force as is necessary. You have the right to the safety and privacy of your own body. You have the right to fight for it.

☆ If the Attacker Has a Weapon

- Do not panic. You are not helpless against a weapon.
- Assess the gravity of the danger.
- Do not get any closer to an attacker with a knife or club.
- Choose a response that will keep you as safe as possible, not only for the moment but for as long as possible.
- Unless you are convinced he will kill you instantly if you don't comply, do not get into a car with an attacker.

☆ The One-Minute Self-defense Workout

Begin by saying, "I am strong. I can take care of myself."
- Three eye strikes
- Three palm heel strikes
- Three punches to the throat
- Three hammer fists
- Three elbow strikes
- Three kicks to the knee

Do these on the right side first, then on the left. End by saying, "I am strong. I can take care of myself."

Self-defense moves are even more effective when used in combinations. For a slightly longer and more advanced work-out, try doing this series of combinations:

Begin by saying, "I am strong, I can take care of myself."
- Eye strike (right hand), right elbow strike to jaw.
- Palm heel strike to nose (right hand), left elbow strike, right kick to knee.
- Grab left shoulder with both hands, knee strike to the groin, left elbow strike.
- Grab left shoulder with your right hand, right kick to knee, left elbow strike.

Repeat three times. End by saying, "I am strong. I can take care of myself."

12

Increasing Physical Strength

The goal of any successful self-defense strategy is to get to a place of safety as quickly as possible. This book offers many suggestions for how you can maneuver to where you can run to people and safety. Now it's time to talk about the running itself.

Let's be realistic. Our best strategy for avoiding rape is in running away. Unless we have a physical disability that prevents us from running, we need to depend on our legs and stamina to get us away from danger. We may have to run a city block or a country mile, but in either case we had better get used to running.

A friend of mine is both a black belt in karate and a long-distance runner. Although she cannot spar with the same speed and strength as some of the bigger and more skilled karate students, she is very effective when she spars because she has incredible stamina from her long-distance training. She simply moves so she won't get hit and waits for her opponent to get tired. Then she strikes back.

184 A LIFE WITHOUT FEAR

> **"Great ideas originate in the muscles."—Thomas Edison**

The Importance of Exercise

Running requires strength in the legs and lower body, and stamina. Upper body strength, pitifully neglected in most American women, is also an important tool in successful self-defense. The physical responses we may have to use will be even more effective if we can put some muscle behind them.

You don't have to be a long-distance runner, a body builder, or a black belt in karate to have the strength and endurance to defend yourself successfully. However, it is important that you be in shape. Exercise will increase your strength, will help you run when you need to, and will make you feel and look more alive.

Many women do not like to exercise. There is no greater incentive, though, for getting and staying in shape than that it may save your life. A rapist looks for someone who is lethargic and sluggish, not someone fit and alert. The act of exercising daily can be a tremendous deterrent to the possibility of sexual assault.

Even though you may not particularly enjoy exercise or feel that you have the time for it, you must take at least twenty minutes four times a week to work out. Do it at the same time of the day so that it becomes routine for you. If you are a morning person, get up a little earlier and take a brisk walk for twenty minutes before you shower. If you need to unwind in the evening, go to the health club or run after you get home from work. It's no longer a matter of *if* you are going to exercise; it is a matter of when you do it and what you do. Regular exercise will change your life, for it will give you a feeling of being in control of your life and will help you attain a life without fear.

Football vs. Conversation

Women have many reasons for hesitating to participate in sports. Many of these reasons have to do with how we were raised and how we are raising our daughters.

In our culture, boys and girls are raised differently and are supported and awarded for different kinds of skills. Girls are awarded for being sweet, pretty, quiet, and giving; boys are applauded when they are assertive, skilled at athletics, independent, and strong.

Think back to when you were in elementary school, and try to remember what the school playground was like at recess. If it was like mine, the girls sat around in the shade of the big oak tree by the corner of the building, trying to stay out of Mrs. Anderson's way. She always made us go out and "get some exercise, it's good for you."

The boys were always in the middle of the hot, dusty yard playing football, kickball, or baseball, depending on the season.

We girls sometimes played four-square, but what we liked to do best was sit around and talk. We talked about the boys, each other, the teachers, but always we talked. And we loved it because it made us feel as though we were all best friends.

The boys didn't talk. They yelled at each other, gave orders to each other, argued about the score, and tried to impress the girls by showing how fast they could run or how far they could hit the ball.

According to Deborah Tannen's book *You Just Don't Understand—Women and Men in Conversation,* boys tend to play outside in large groups with a clear-cut hierarchy. The leader tells the other boys what to do, and they do it. Boys actually play games where keeping score is necessary or desirable, and they are focused on the physical.

On the other hand, girls tend to play in smaller groups where status is gained by having close relationships with other girls. A best friend is a necessity, the center of a girl's social life. Girls are more concerned with being liked and often sit together and talk.

"Though all humans need both intimacy and independence, women tend to focus on the first, men on the second."
—Deborah Tanner, *You Just Don't Understand—Men and Women in Conversation*

Because of the influence of these early years, men and women reach adulthood with different ideas and perspectives about their bodies. Women tend to view their bodies with a critical eye. We don't pay much attention to the muscles or lack thereof, but we tend to focus on the paunch in our stomachs or the love handles around our waists. It seems to matter more to us how we look rather than how we feel or what we can do with our bodies. Not many women I know challenge each other to an arm wrestling contest or a do-or-die match on the racquetball court.

As a whole, women are ignorant of the potential of their physical power. Discovering the strength of our bodies and mastering a sport or physical skill can be an exciting adventure, particularly for a woman who has never done this.

Gloria Steinem wrote in *Revolution from Within,* "For women to enjoy physical strength is a collective revolution." And what a joyous revolution it is!

Exercise and sports help us become better acquainted with our bodies and with our limitations and potential. The new emphasis on exercise, the increase in the number of girls' athletic teams, and the tremendous popularity of aerobics classes at health clubs are allowing women to appreciate the delight of becoming strong.

Encouraging girls to become active in sports at an early age will help them develop lifestyles that are healthy both physically and emotionally. Sports will help them develop their strong, assertive selves, which is crucial to their safety and independence.

The tragedy of our culture is that we don't encourage well-rounded individuals who are strong *and* sweet, assertive *and* giving, and equally at home with the physical and the emotional. It is a disservice to boys and girls.

Staying in Shape and Staying Safe

When we look at the characteristics that lead to increased safety, we can achieve many of them by leading a physically active life. Regular exercise results in many benefits that will also help us stay safe, such as:

- Being alert
- Increased awareness
- Increased endurance
- Increased self-esteem
- Greater physical strength
- An attitude of energy and self-confidence.

Although any number of sports and exercises will produce the results needed, some will be better suited to your lifestyle than others. Although the National Mental Health Institute found that girls who had played football growing up had a greater success at defending themselves than girls who did not, playing football is not necessarily a viable means of getting exercise for many of us. The kind of exercise you get is not nearly as important as the fact that you get up and *do* something.

"Women who avoided being raped were substantially more likely to engage in sports regularly: Almost half did so compared with approximately one fourth of the raped women."—Pauline B. Bart and Patricia H. O'Brien, *Stopping Rape*

There no doubt is a correlation between being active in sports and exercise and avoiding rape. Although it is impossible to say that if you exercise three or four times a week or play soccer, basketball, or volleyball twice a week you will never be raped, participating in sports will reduce the risk, while providing other physical and psychological benefits.

"But I Don't Have Time to Exercise"

Everyone has a favorite excuse for not working out. Maybe it's too cold or too hot. Maybe you don't have anyone to work out with, or maybe the health club is too crowded. Maybe you don't have the right clothes to wear, or the right shoes, or the right place, or enough energy. Maybe you feel that if you have any extra time, you should spend it with your children, husband, or boyfriend.

It's easy to justify spending time doing something—*anything*—else.

You might lull yourself into thinking that if you ever really needed to run or defend yourself, you could. How do you know that unless you try it? And how do you know how far you would have to run? And how fast? If you've never been attacked before, how do you *really* know how you'll react?

People react differently in times of stress and terror. Many of us are hit with a tremendous surge of adrenalin, and at first we feel superhuman strength. But this doesn't last. The body quickly overloads, and we soon experience an adrenalin dump, resulting in lethargy and the sensation of time moving at an extraordinarily slow pace.

When faced with danger, other people feel weak in the knees and seem to freeze in fright.

If you expect your body to work for you in times of stress, you must condition it in times of relaxation. Let's face it. If you eat cheesecake every night for dinner and the only exercise you get is opening the refrigerator door, your body is not going to be a lean, mean, fighting machine.

You don't have to be an Olympic athlete to make self-defense work for you. However, the better shape you are in, the harder you can hit and the faster you can run.

In addition to increased strength and stamina, keeping in shape and getting regular exercise results in your being more alert and aware and being able to function at higher energy levels, all of which will aid you in keeping safe on the street, at home, at work, or anywhere else.

"I'm So Mad, I'm Going to Explode"

If you're attacked, your first feeling probably will be fear. For most of us, this is almost always followed by pure, unadulterated rage and anger.

When you get angry, your body actually goes through a series of chemical changes. These changes are left over from the early years of the history of humankind when we depended on our "fight or flight" reaction to survive. Generally, in a fit of anger we have increased heartbeat and blood pressure, higher skin temperatures, and fatty acids are put into the bloodstream for use as fuel. All of this prepares the body for action.

If no action is taken and we simply stand and fume, the pressure on the heart and circulatory system is tremendous. We really might explode. If we can learn to use this chemical reaction through physical exertion, our strength will be increased and we can be assured that this is a healthy, positive way to expel the anger.

Another great benefit of regular exercise is in helping to control anger and stress. For certain personality types, anger can be potentially very dangerous. If you get angry often, this can multiply your chances of getting high blood pressure and heart disease.

In terms of defending yourself, this chemical reaction can be of critical importance. If you can turn a feeling of fear into one of anger, your body will help you. But this is not always easy. You have to make a conscious decision to be angry, not afraid.

If you are attacked, you have to control your body first; then you have to take charge of the situation. Take a deep breath. Tell yourself, I'm not scared. I'm mad. I am furious. How dare he do this to me! As you convince yourself, and subsequently your body, that you are experiencing anger, not fear, your chemical reactions will change dramatically. You will change from a "frozen" state, where it is hard to move and hard to breathe, to a state of great strength and power.

Taking action physically will also help put emotional distance between you and your attacker. In other words, if you can get angry and vent your anger physically, you will begin to feel a sense of control over the situation. This will help not only physically, but also in your emotional and psychological recovery.

Getting Started

Exercise does not have to be a complicated affair. Your exercise program can begin with something as simple as walking around the block.

If you are over thirty-five or have not exercised for a while, make sure you check with a doctor before you start any strenuous exercise program.

One of the benefits of exercising regularly is a feeling of accomplishment. To enhance this, keep track of your exercise routine and watch the improvement you make. You'll be astounded at your program.

You don't need anything fancy or complicated to get started exercising. If you think you might want to get involved with a health club or a karate studio, or any other kind of organized exercise program, that's great! Don't wait to begin exercising until you do it, though. That will simply postpone your start, and you need to begin now.

The easiest exercises to do on your own, at home, by yourself, are walking, running, and simple floor exercises. Everyone knows how to walk and has a place to do it, even if you have to jog in place in front of the television.

Walking/Running

Running, jogging, and walking all are excellent aerobic activities. Anybody can do them any time, anywhere. It will be helpful to carry a watch with a second hand so you can time yourself. If you are unused to exercising, start slowly so you won't get sore or discouraged.

Week 1. Put on a pair of comfortable shoes and walk briskly for ten minutes. Keep your back straight, tighten your stomach muscles, and keep alert. Do this every day for the first week.

If you feel a little tightness in your legs, that's OK. It shows that you're working those muscles. Getting out and walking again will actually help loosen them up.

Week 2. Begin adding more time to your routine. Increase it to twenty minutes, but continue to walk slowly as you gain strength.

Week 3. Now is the time to start pushing yourself a little. Your goal is for a *brisk* walk so that you feel slightly out of breath during the entire twenty minutes.

Week 4 and the rest of your life. Continue the walking routine. You may want to increase the time to thirty minutes or longer, and you may want to increase your speed to keep yourself challenged. The important thing is that you keep it up.

Walking is a wonderful exercise. Normally it does not strain your muscles, and it makes you feel alert and alive. You will quickly come to enjoy your daily walk and will begin to look forward to it. It will become your time to unwind, to think, dream, and plan.

Running

If you have not exercised much lately and want to begin running, do so gradually until your body gets used to it. Begin by alternating walking and running. Do this routine at least four times a week.

Week 1. Walk briskly for five minutes, run or jog for one minute, and then walk again. Repeat this four times, ending with a one-minute cool-down walk.

Week 2. Continue to alternate running and walking, but add time to the running. Walk five minutes, run three minutes, and repeat four times. This will add six minutes to your exercise routine.

Week 3. Continue with the same routine.

Week 4. You're probably ready to add more running. Begin with a five-minute warm-up walk; run for five minutes; walk one minute.

Repeat two more times, ending with a five-minute cool-down walk.

Week 5. Begin with a five-minute warm up walk. Run for ten minutes; walk for one minute; run for ten minutes. End with five-minute cool-down walk

Week 6. You're really running now. You probably won't need your one-minute walks. Begin with a five-minute warm-up walk; run or jog for twenty minutes. End with a five-minute cool-down walk.

Continue. If you ever get really sore or your muscles feel fatigued, go back to a walking/running routine, or walk briskly for a few days until your body heals. Do not stop exercising. Just slow it down.

Sit-ups and Push-ups

Old-fashioned but effective, these two basic exercises, if done regularly, will quickly increase your overall strength. Women are particularly negligent about building upper body strength. Don't worry about building massive muscles; unless you go on a strenuous weightlifting regimen, chances are pretty slim that you will bulk up with a lot of muscle. These exercises work lean muscles, building strength without bulk.

Sit-ups. Always do sit-ups with bent knees to protect your back. If you are a novice, try starting in a sitting position with your knees bent. Slowly lower your body to the floor. As you get stronger, lie on your back with knees at a 45-degree angle, hands folded across your chest, fingertips touching opposite shoulders. Come up, touching elbows to opposite knees. These will be easier to do if a partner holds your feet. You can also slip your feet under a sofa to hold them down. It is not necessary, it's just a bit easier and more comfortable. If you need more of a challenge, hold a book or weight to your chest as you do these exercises.

You should do sit-ups every day. They increase the abdominal muscles, which are important muscles for every kind of activity and exercise we do. Strong stomach muscles will also help protect a weak back.

Note: If these sit-ups hurt your back, check with your doctor for special abdominal exercises that protect your back.

Day 1. Begin by lying on the floor, knees bent, arms crossed across your chest. Tighten your stomach muscles and slowly raise up to touch your right elbow to your left knee. Lower yourself to the floor, still keeping your stomach muscles tight. Raise up again, touching your left elbow to your right knee. Repeat for a total of ten sit-ups.

Day 2. Repeat.

Day 3. Repeat.

Day 4. Add five sit-ups to the routine.

As your strength increases, keep adding to the total number of sit-ups that you do until you can easily do fifty every day.

Keep track of your progress in a notebook. If you stick with it and do them every day, you'll be surprised at how quickly you can increase the number.

Push-ups. Women *can* do push-ups. If you do them regularly, you will be surprised at how quickly you can build up the total number you can do. If you are a novice, try doing a static push-up. Hold your body as straight as possible in a push-up position (toes and hands). Then try to do one full push-up. Bend your arms, but keep your body straight until your nose is two inches from the floor, then slowly straighten your arms. Make sure that your body stays straight and that you don't stick your buttocks up in the air, or let your stomach drag toward the floor. Do as many as you can from your hands and toes. "Girl" push-ups, from the knees and the hands, have limited usefulness.

If you can't do a single push-up, don't worry. Many women can't. Hang in there, though, because you will be able to do it and a good push-up is a wonderful accomplishment.

Week 1

Day 1. Get in the push-up position and hold it for a count of five. Relax by putting a knee down for support, and then get back up into the push-up position. Repeat three times.

Day 2. Repeat, but add another count of five.

Day 3. Repeat.

Day 4. Repeat.

Day 5. Hold the push-up position for a count of four, and then slightly bend your arms and straighten them slowly. Include this "dip" for each count of five.

Day 6. Repeat, making the "dip" slightly deeper.

Day 7. Repeat.

Week 2

Day 1. Get in the push-up position and do one full push-up. Relax for a count of five. Get back in position, do another full push-up. Relax and repeat two more times.

Continue to repeat this routine, gradually decreasing the time between push-ups. When you can do four push-ups without relaxing in between, gradually add to the total number. Push yourself to do a little more every time.

Keep track of your progress.

Sit-ups	*Push-ups*
Day 1 _____	Day 1 _____
Day 2 _____	Day 2 _____
Day 3 _____	Day 3 _____
Day 4 _____	Day 4 _____
Day 5 _____	Day 5 _____

Weight Lifting: For fast, measurable results, try lifting weights. You don't have to go to a weight room or a health club to do this. There are plenty of objects lying around the house that you can use for weights. Take an old plastic detergent bottle and fill it with sand or water. Grasp it by the handle or neck, and lift slowly. If it's too heavy at first, dump out some of the sand or water.

If you prefer to purchase ready-made weights, you can buy a small set of fairly inexpensive dumbbells at a sporting goods store or even a discount store. These usually come in sets of three-, five-, and eight-pound weights.

You can do a variety of easy arm exercises with weights. Do them in sets of eight. Rest at least thirty seconds, and then do another set. Gradually increase the weight and the number of repetitions.

Week 1. Begin with three sets of eight repetitions, using a light enough weight so that you can do it comfortably. Repeat three or four times a week.

Week 2. Increase the total number so you are doing three sets of ten repetitions.

Week 3. Increase so you are doing three sets of twelve repetitions.

Week 4. Gradually begin to add weight. Continue with three sets of twelve repetitions.

Exercises:

- Grasp the weights, palms up, arms hanging by your sides. Slowly bend your elbows, lifting the weights toward your shoulders. Slowly lower them back to a straight arm position.
- With your arms hanging down by your sides again, turn your palms downward and lift the weights with straight arms out to the sides until your hands are even with your shoulders. Slowly lower them until they touch your sides. Repeat.
- Same as above, only lift the weights straight out in front of you instead of to the sides. Repeat.
- Bend your elbows and rest your hands and the weights on

your shoulders, palms facing in. Slowly raise your arms straight above your head. Slowly lower to your shoulders again. Repeat.

Weightlifting progress:

Day 1: Exercise 1 _____ pounds _____ sets of __
       Exercise 2 _____
       Exercise 3 _____
       Exercise 4 _____

Day 2: Exercise 1 _____ pounds _____ sets of __
       Exercise 2 _____
       Exercise 3 _____
       Exercise 4 _____

And so forth.

If you build up your exercise program to where you run or walk at least twenty minutes three or four times a week and do sit-ups, push-ups, or weights three or four times a week, you will be well on your way to fitness—and safety.

Unfortunately, the body does not store fitness. To keep the benefits of staying fit, you must continue to exercise. Exercise must be part of your lifestyle from now on.

"Most research indicates that body conditioning acquired after a four-week training program is lost within two weeks if training is discontinued completely."—Roberta Stokes and Clancy Moore, *Personal Fitness and You*

Sports and Classes

Aerobics Classes

Aerobics classes come in many different guises. Step, Jazzercise, funk, hi-low impact, and body sculpting are all names of classes offered at most health clubs or Ys. Each offers different benefits, but all have the advantage of getting you moving, in tune with your body, and in shape. An aerobics class also has the advantage of being a social activity. It is fun to exercise with friends, and you'll be surprised at how much easier it is to work with a group than it is to work on your own. The collective spirit will help move you through the class and make the time go quickly.

Sports

Just as you can do countless exercises to improve your overall fitness, you can get involved in numerous sports that will also get you in shape and keep you fit, alert, and alive.

Nearly every woman involved in sports will tell you hers is the best—the most exciting, the most fun, the best exercise. And they're all right! Whatever captures your interest or keeps you actively involved, do it.

Karate

In reference to self-defense, however, karate or other martial arts will be of the greatest direct benefit. Not only will you learn techniques that are directly applicable in self-defense, you will learn about focus, speed, intensity, and inner strength.

Karate will build your self-confidence faster than any other sport I know of. It is exciting to learn how strong you are and how well you can control your body. Hitting air targets with full power is also a magnificent way to relieve tension. It is a sport where intensity is emphasized and encouraged.

Karate is a very goal-oriented sport. At each different belt level you have a specific amount of work to do. As you master different techniques, you will progress through the ranks and will be awarded with different colors of belts to indicate where you are on your karate journey.

The martial arts are very spiritually oriented as well, allowing you to combine inner strength and physical power.

Whatever sport or exercise program you choose to participate in will reward you many times over. In exercise, as in everything else, the amount of time and energy you put into it will determine how much you get out of it. Increasing your fitness level will make you feel better and will help your safety and enhance your chance of survival in an attack.

As you learn to use your physical and inner strength, you will begin to realize your potential for caring for yourself. The gift of fitness is the gift of self-confidence.

IN A NUTSHELL

1. If our best strategy to avoid rape is to run away, we had better learn to run fast.
2. Boys and girls in our culture are raised differently. Boys accentuate the physical; girls place emphasis on relationships.
3. Exercise and sports help women become better aware of our own bodies—our limitations *and* our potential.
4. Regular exercise results in benefits that also help keep us safe, such as being more alert, increased awareness and endurance, and greater physical strength.
5. There is correlation between being active in sports and exercise and in avoiding rape.
6. You don't have to be an Olympic athlete to make self-defense work for you; but the better shape you are in, the harder you can hit and the faster you can run.
7. Anger triggers physiological responses from the body that can be used to your advantage in thwarting an attack.
8. The gift of fitness is the gift of self-confidence.

13

Safety Tips for Everywhere

I n the mid-eighties Robert Fulghum wrote an enormously popular book called *Everything I Ever Needed to Know, I Learned in Kindergarten*. The same basic principles that Fulghum proposed in his book could be used to keep you safe.

Increasing your chances of staying safe and preventing sexual assault are based on common sense. You can greatly lessen your chances of being attacked by following those simple rules that your mom told you every time you left the house:

Use the buddy system. Stay away from dark places. Don't talk to strangers. Don't ever ride with someone you don't know. Lock the doors. Carry enough change to make a phone call. Know where you're going, and don't get lost. And don't ever, ever, ever hitchhike. It's all good advice for anyone from age 3 to 103.

Many attacks from strangers occur when we are stranded because the car ran out of gas or quit for some other reason, or because we got lost and had to stop for directions. Remember that good safety practices involve being self-sufficient and not having to depend on others for transportation or telling us how to get home.

If you feel strongly that something is not quite right, get to a telephone and call the police. Don't be shy about doing this. It is their job to protect citizens, and they prefer preventing crime to cleaning up after one. Arrange to have someone close to you contacted in case of an emergency.

Try to vary your routine from time to time. Daily patterns are easily learned by assailants. Leave for and return from work at different times. If you take the dog for a walk every day, sometimes do it in the morning, sometimes during lunch. Keep a would-be assailant guessing where and when you will show up.

Discuss the following safety tips with your family, including the special section on kids and safety. Read it carefully, and talk to your children about staying safe.

When You're in Your Car

- Keep your car in good running order.
- Do not let your gas tank get more than three-fourths empty.
- If your car stops, get out, raise the hood, get back in the car, lock the doors, and wait. When someone stops, only roll the window down far enough to talk to him. Ask him to go to the nearest phone and call for help. Do not get out of the car.
- If you see another motorist on the road who needs help, *do not stop.* If you want to help, go to the nearest exit or phone and call the police.
- If you have a flat tire, go ahead and drive slowly to the closest safe place. A bent rim is a small price to pay for your safety.
- If someone signals that you are having car trouble, do not stop until you have reached a safe, lighted spot with people around. Then you can check it out.
- If you are involved in a minor accident that you feel was done on purpose, stay in the car and talk through the win-

dow. Do not get out unless the police come. If necessary, drive to the police station.

- Keep an emergency kit in your car with flashlight, flares, tow chain, first aid kit, spare tire, and a *help* sign.
- Know where you are going and how to get back. Keep a current map in your car of areas you will be traveling.
- When you are driving, always keep your car doors locked and windows rolled up. Attackers have been known to jump into unlocked cars while they are stopped at red lights.
- If you are stopped at a light and someone starts to mess with your car in any manner (washing the windows, going for the hubcaps, for instance), honk the horn and drive off if possible.
- If you have a convertible, do not leave the top down when driving at night or if you are driving in an unsafe area.
- Always lock your car when you leave it.
- Stay anonymous on the road. Don't indulge in a personalized license plate.
- *Never, ever hitchhike or pick up hitchhikers.*
- If you suspect someone is following you, drive to the police station or to a busy service station with people around to help you.
- Keep a current telephone directory under the front seat. With it you can find an address without asking a stranger, call a wrecker service, or get a phone number in the safety of your car.

Parking Your Car

- Always leave your car in the safest place possible. This is not a time or place to scrimp and save money. Your safety should be a top financial priority. If you can, leave it at a parking lot with an attendant. Park as close as you can to your destination, and park under lights. If you leave the car during daylight hours and plan to return after dark, don't forget to park it where lights will illuminate your car at night.

- Always lock your car when you park it.
- When you return to your vehicle, have the key to the door lock in your hand and be ready to get into your car as quickly as possible.
- Before getting into your car, check to make sure that it has not been tampered with. Check the back seat.
- Avoid leaving valuables in the car.
- When you have to leave a key with a parking attendant, leave only the ignition key, not the key to the trunk or your house or apartment.
- Keep your ignition key separate from your house key.
- Try to walk with someone else to your car. If you came in separate vehicles, the two of you can then drive to the other car.
- Make notes if necessary, but always be absolutely certain you know where you left your car.
- When walking to your car, avoid walking close to parked cars or other places where people might be hiding.
- Never hide a key in a parked car. If you thought of a good place to hide it, someone else could think of it, too.
- Unless there is an attendant, avoid parking underground if possible. If this is not possible, at least remove shoes that make a lot of noise when returning to your car.

Public Transportation

- Avoid being the lone passenger in a subway car.
- If you are being hassled physically or verbally on a bus or subway and other commuters are nearby, turn around and verbally confront your attacker. Call attention to him.
- When waiting for a bus or taxi, stand under the light but not too close to the edge of the street.
- Be alert while waiting for public transportation. Do not read a book or newspaper. It divides your attention.
- Do not sit right next to the door. Sometimes thieves will dash in, grab a purse, and be off as the doors close. When possible, sit on an aisle seat so you can get up easily.
- Hold on to your belongings firmly, holding a purse or briefcase in your lap or wedged between your legs.

- If possible, don't carry a purse. If you have to carry a purse, use a shoulder bag that you can easily hold on to, or wear it across your body. Wear clothes with deep, tight pockets to carry essential items.
- Do not sleep on public transportation.
- When riding a bus, sit close to the driver if you can.

When You Are Walking

- Be observant at all times.
- Know your route, and don't take shortcuts unless you know exactly where they go and that they travel through safe areas.
- Whenever you can, walk with someone else.
- Walk with your head held high and with an air of confidence.
- Walk close to the curb and avoid doorways, alleys, shrubs, and parked cars.
- Dress so you won't call attention to yourself. Avoid flashy or skimpy clothes and expensive jewelry.
- *Do not stop to engage in conversation with strangers on the street. Do not give directions or answer questions.*
- If approached by someone in a car, *do not get any closer to the car.* Turn and walk in the other direction.
- If you think you are being followed, check it out. Quicken your pace or stop to do some window-shopping. If you determine you are being followed, try not to look nervous. Walk confidently to the nearest safe place (store or office building), and call the police. *Do not walk home if you think you are being followed.*
- Plan your route home as you would a strategic defense plan. Know what stores or offices could offer you safety if you needed it. Know what time they close. Choose an alternate route if you need to.
- Be able to move quickly. Don't overload yourself with books or packages. Be conscious of what you wear. If you always wear straight skirts or jeans so tight you can't move easily, this will hamper you if you need to defend yourself. Be particularly conscious of your shoes. Wear shoes that

you can run in or at least kick off easily. Think about this the next time you buy a pair of shoes.

- If you are approached on the street by someone demanding money, jewelry, or whatever, quickly determine the level of potential danger. If you believe this is a threat to your safety in any way, give him whatever he demands. No material possession is worth being raped or killed.
- Never count money on the street. Do it in the privacy of a bank or office or in your home.
- Always walk facing traffic.
- If you are being followed by a car, turn around and walk in the opposite direction.

Keeping Safe at Home

- Be able to get into your home quickly and easily. Have the door key out and ready when you arrive.
- If you have an automatic garage door opener, watch in the rearview mirror until the door has closed behind you, making sure no one slips in.
- If you are being followed, do not go straight home. Go to a safe place, and call the police.
- If someone is in your house when you go in, don't corner him. Give him a psychological and physical out. Say something like, "Oh, I didn't expect a repairman until tomorrow."
- Know the area around your home. Know where an intruder might hide, and do a quick check of these places if you drive in alone at night.
- If you suspect that someone is in your house when you get home (a door is opened or a window broken), do not go in. Go to a neighbor's house, and call the police. Wait until they get there before you go in.
- *Do not open your door to strangers.* Know who is at the door before you open it.
- Be cautious of uniformed men at the door. Unless you have called for a repair or delivery man, do not let one in the house. If they insist they have legitimate business there,

make them wait outside until you have called their company to verify.

- Keep your doors locked when you are away and when you are home.
- Do not allow a stranger to enter a locked building behind you. If he has a legitimate reason to be there, he can get in on his own.
- Keep a telephone by your bed for emergencies.
- Have a safety route planned for your home in case of fire or intruders.
- Place a deadbolt on your bedroom door so if someone comes into your home, you can go there, lock yourself in, and call for help.
- If you have to be away for a few days, get timers for the lights so you give the appearance of being home.
- When you are on vacation, get a friend or neighbor to come by to check on the house and make it look lived in.
- When you will be gone for several days, make sure you stop mail and newspaper. Papers in the driveway or stacked up at your mailbox are a sure sign that you are out of town.

On the Phone

- Do not answer the phone with your name. If a stranger asks who it is, ask him to identify himself first.
- Be careful whom you give your number to. When in doubt, get their phone number and call them instead.
- Have important phone numbers readily available.
- If you get an obscene phone call, hang up immediately. If he calls back, blow directly into the phone with a shrill whistle.
- If prank callers persist, report it to the phone company or to the police.
- Do not leave personal information on your answering machine. Identify yourself with just your phone number.
- List only your last name and initials in the phone book.
- Keep a phone by your bed for emergencies.

Keeping Your Home Safe

- Do not hide a house key in an obvious place. Avoid leaving a key outside.
- Do not leave a note on the door saying that you are gone or when you will return.
- Safety is a good investment. Live in as safe a place as you can afford.
- Make sure you have good locks on your doors. Use deadbolts.
- Exterior doors should be made of solid wood or metal. All exterior doors should have a peephole.
- Avoid locks that can be reached by breaking glass or wooden panels.
- Keep garage doors closed and locked at all times.
- Only give house or apartment keys to those who really need them.
- Invest in an alarm system, and check it monthly to make sure it works.
- Make sure that there is adequate lighting around your home or apartment. If you are going to be home alone at night, keep the lights on all night.
- Keep all ladders inside.
- Keep shrubbery trimmed below window level.
- Take down tree limbs or trellises that would allow easy access to upper-level windows.
- Know names and phone numbers of neighbors.

Safety Tips for Children

- Talk to your children about where to go for help. Talk to them about going to authority figures, such as the police. Unfortunately, it will also be important to warn them not to trust someone, such as a teacher, simply because he or she is in a position of authority.
- Tell them not to talk with strangers or anyone they do not know well.
- If a stranger asks them a question, tell them you said they do not have to answer.

- Make sure children understand that they *should not open the door for people they do not know.*
- Make sure your children know how to get in touch with you or with another adult if they need help.
- Always know where your children are.
- Require that your children use the buddy system or walk in groups when possible.
- Have your children carry an emergency quarter or memorize your telephone calling card number. Make sure they know how to use a pay phone.
- Make sure your children know their neighborhood and the route to school thoroughly.
- If your child rides a bike, set up specific routes and boundaries where he or she is allowed to ride. Have your child wear a helmet when riding on the street.
- Keep current pictures of your children.
- Young children should not be left alone in the house or car.
- Thoroughly check out day care centers or baby-sitters before you leave your child.
- Make sure your children know how to call 911. Tell them to stay on the phone line until the call has been verified.
- Make sure your children know they should not leave school with anyone else unless you approve first.
- *Listen to your children! Talk with them about important things and trivial things as well. If you lay a firm foundation of trust and love with your children when they are young, you will be able to communicate with them throughout their lives.*

Conclusion:
The Hero's Journey

Facing the reality of rape is painful whether you have survived a sexual assault, are a friend of someone who has been raped, or are a victim of the fear the near epidemic of rape has brought to women. It is important to acknowledge that rape in this country is widespread, and unless we recognize that all women are at risk *because they are women,* we will make little progress, if any, in combating this outrage.

To stop rape means that we need to grow into the women we are capable of becoming. We must build our self-esteem and learn to be graciously assertive so we can control our own lives. We will do that. We will find the skills to communicate clearly and effectively so we can say no and have people believe us. We will take care of our bodies so we are strong and fit, ready to flee from danger or fight for our lives.

To accomplish this will take courage, because women generally have not been raised to be independent, assertive individuals. It will take courage to fight for our safety, to be open and honest in our relationships; and it will take real heroes to move from what we know to a richer and more mature way of living.

In no way does this mean that we have to do it alone. Many women have found that the best way to grow and mature is within the safety of a loving relationship with a man. Others have found the strength to grow from the support of friends and family. Still others brave this journey alone.

But the fact remains that our inner growth is essential to our safety. Growth is difficult, but the alternative—allowing the situation to remain unchanged—is unthinkable.

We all are in the trenches in this war against rape, and it is not easy. It is not pretty, and it is not fun; but it is absolutely essential for our very safety that we remain in this fight together.

With increased knowledge and understanding about rape and sexual assault comes responsibility to share this information. You already know too much to turn your back. Take what you know, and start talking. Talk to a friend, talk to your mother, talk to your sister. Together we will talk loudly enough to be heard, for every woman deserves a life without fear.

Selected Bibliography

Acquaintance Rape and Sexual Assault Prevention Training Manual, by Andrea Parrot. Department of Human Service Studies, Cornell University: Ithaca, New York, 1990.

Against Our Will, by Susan Brownmiller. Bantam Books: New York, 1975.

The Cinderella Complex: Women's Hidden Fear of Independence, by Colette Dowling. Summit Books: New York, 1981.
A very good book explaining how culture and upbringing teach women to keep waiting for that fairy godmother. Important in that it helps women realize how crucial it is for us to take responsibility for our own lives and welfare.

Fear or Freedom, by Susan Smith. Mother Courage Press: Racine, Wisc., 1986.
A good, but wordy, treatise on rape and self-defense.

The Female Fear, by Margaret T. Gordon and Stephanie Riger. The Free Press: New York, 1989.
Based on a large study funded by the National Center for the Prevention and Control of Rape. Results of over 300 interviews. Discusses the prevalence of the fear of rape.

Feminist Fatale, by Paula Kamen. Donald I. Fine, Inc.: New York, 1991.

This is an excellent voice declaring where the feminist movement is in the early 1990s. The author (and all women interviewed) are in their twenties and give frank opinions on women at home, in the work force, on abortion, child care, and many other women's issues.

Fight Back: Feminist Resistance to Male Violence, edited by Frederique Delacoste and Felice Neweman. Cleis Press: Minneapolis, Minn., 1981.

Her Wits About Her: Self-defense Success Stories by Women, edited by Denise Caignon and Gail Groves. Harper and Row: New York, 1987.

This is a compilation of true life stories written by women who were victims of rape or attempted rape. It brings the problem close to home but is encouraging because these stories are about survivors.

How to Be an Assertive (Not Aggressive) Woman, by Jean Baer. Penguin Books: New York, 1976.

Gives some good advice about being gracefully assertive.

I Never Called It Rape, by Robin Warshaw. Ms. Foundation/ Sarah Lazin Books, Harper and Row: New York, 1988.

The Bible for information on date and campus rape. This is based on an extensive study funded by the *Ms.* magazine foundation. Full of statistics and case studies, it presents a very clear and concise overview of the problems of date and acquaintance rape. Geared toward college-aged women.

Invisible Wounds: Crime Victims Speak, by Shelley Neiderbach. Harrington Park Press: New York, 1986.

A wonderful guide for understanding the effects that violent crime can have on a person. This provides a good tool for helping yourself overcome the aftermath of violent crime or helping someone close to you.

Learned Optimism: How to Change Your Mind and Life, by Martin E. P. Seligman. Pocket Books: New York, 1990.

Author explains the detrimental effects of pessimism and how you can actually practice to change your attitude about life. Discusses how optimism can help you in many areas including school, sports, health, and family relationships. In terms of self-defense, a pessimist is more likely to display victim characteristics.

Male and Female Realities: Understanding the Opposite Sex, by Joe Tanebaum. R. J. Erdmann: San Marcos, Calif., 1990.

An in-depth discussion of how men and women differ. There are undeniable differences and a greater understanding of these differences may make communication a little easier.

Nobody Told Me It Was Rape, by Caren Adams and Jennifer Fay. Impact Publishers: Santa Cruz, Calif., 1984.

Probably the best booklet available about talking to teenagers and adolescents about rape. Includes a frank discussion of the problem, suggestions about how to approach the subject with your child, and sample conversations.

One-minute Self-esteem: Caring for Yourself and Others, by Candace Semigran. Bantam Books: New York, 1988.

A small book that briefly discusses personal fears that keep one from gaining self-esteem. Easy to read and a few good exercises but not much meat here.

The Psychology of Self-esteem, by Nathaniel Branden. Bantam Books: New York, 1971.

A good overview of the importance of self-esteem.

Safe in the Streets: Don't Be a Victim, by Sandra J. Merwin. Book Peddlers: Deephaven, Minn., 1985.

Very good suggestions for staying safe—from walking on the street to keeping your house safe.

The Seven Habits of Highly Effective People, by Stephen Covey. Fireside Press: New York, 1989.

A very important book for anyone who wants to learn to take charge of her own life. Covey offers practical suggestions and exercises on becoming more effective. The book bogs down in the middle, but keep plugging. It's worth it.

Sexual Assault: How to Defend Yourself, by Lena and Marie Howard. Fell Publishers: Hollywood, Fla., 1990.

A good collection of self-defense moves with clear instructions and good illustrations. Lead-in chapters are useful for talking with teens about rape.

Sixth Sense, by Laurie Nadel. Metamorphous Press: New York, 1990.

Goes into detail as to how to recognize and develop your own intuitive powers.

SoftPower!, by Maria Arapakis. Warner Books: New York, 1990.

A very good book for women who are unused to or uncomfortable with assertive action. The author encourages without preaching and paints a strong picture of what you can turn into if you don't stand up for yourself, as well as what you can become if you do. Beneficial for the woman who does not work outside the home in addition to those who pursue a career.

Stopping Rape: Successful Survival Strategies, by Pauline B. Bart and Patricia H. O'Brien. Pergamon Press: Elmsford, N.Y., 1985.

Based on a national mental health study on rape. The authors compiled information about successful strategies used most often by women who experienced rape or attempted rape.

Talking Back to Sexual Pressure, by Elizabeth Powell. CompCare Publishers: Minneapolis, Minn., 1991.

Deals with the problems of women in the work place. Offers advice on how to respond verbally and physically, how to assert yourself and survive in the corporate world.

Toward a New Psychology of Women, by Jean Baker Miller. Beacon Press: Boston, 1986.

Treatise on the need for women to become more assertive and more self-confident.

When I Say No, I Feel Guilty, by Manuel J. Smith. Bantam Books: New York, 1975.

A good book for many women who just can't say no to anyone. Discusses basic assertive rights, communication, and dealings with criticism. The basic point is that you have the right to say no.

Index

Laura Martin is a columnist for the *Atlanta Journal-Constitution* and author of seven books. A graduate of the University of Georgia, she also holds a first-degree black belt in traditional karate and first- and second-degree black belts in American karate. In addition to her writing, she teaches classes for women on the art of self-defense; it was the questions asked by her students that made her realize the need for a book that goes beyond self-defense into the mental toughness and preparedness required for women to prevent sexual assault. Her articles have been published in *National Wildlife* magazine, *Better Homes and Gardens,* and other national magazines. She lives in Atlanta, Georgia, with her son and daughter.